P9-DVP-667

WITHDRAWN

THE

HEAVEN

ON

SEVEN

COOKBOOK

CAUTION! DO NOT TOUCH! CONTENTS MAY EXPLODE!

CAUTION! DO NOT TOUCH

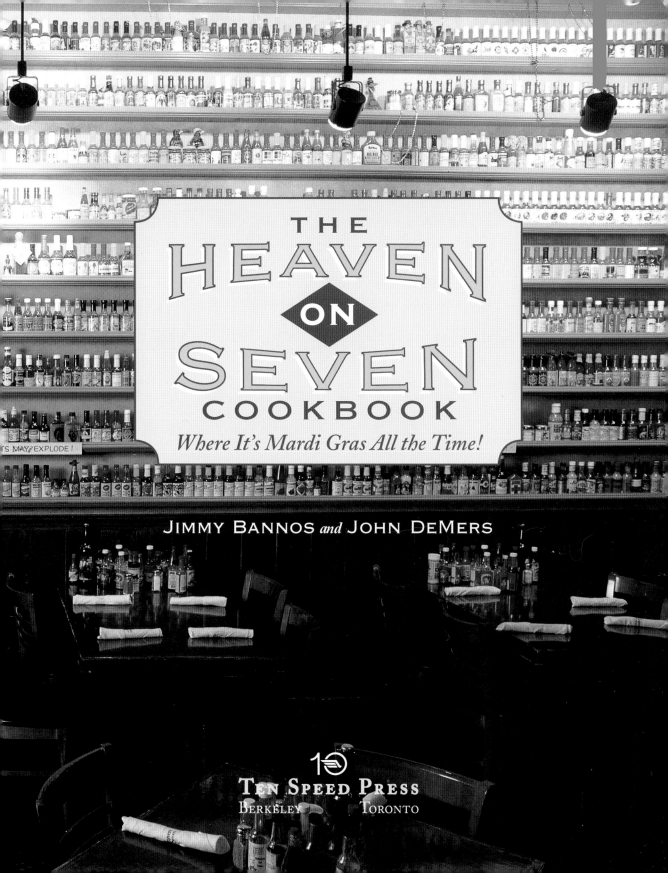

THE
HEAVEN
ON
SEVEN
COOKBOOK

Where It's Mardi Gras All the Time!

JIMMY BANNOS *and* JOHN DEMERS

Ten Speed Press
BERKELEY   TORONTO

39409925

641.59763
BAN

Copyright © 2000 by Jimmy Bannos and John DeMers

All rights reserved. No part of this book may be reproduced in any form, except brief excerpts for the purpose of review, without written permission of the publisher.

Some of the recipes in this book include raw eggs, meat, or fish. When these foods are consumed raw, there is always the risk that bacteria, which is killed by proper cooking, may be present. For this reason, when serving these foods raw, always buy certified salmonella-free eggs and the freshest meat and fish available from a reliable grocer, storing them in the refrigerator until they are served. Because of the health risks associated with the consumption of bacteria that can be present in raw eggs, meat, and fish, these foods should not be consumed by infants, small children, pregnant women, the elderly, or any people who may be immuno-compromised

Book design: Chris Hall
Copyediting: Janet Schilling-Mowery
Photography: Eric Futran, Chicago
Photos on pages v, 2, and 74 provided by the author.
Additional photography: Bill Mahin (pages 99 and 35) and Pamela Bannos (pages 11, 59, and 123)
Food styling: Joan Moravek

Ten Speed Press
Box 7123
Berkeley, California 94707
www.tenspeed.com

Distributed in Australia by Simon & Schuster Australia, in Canada by Ten Speed Press Canada, in New Zealand by Southern Publishers Group, in South Africa by Real Books, in Southeast Asia by Berkeley Books, and in the United Kingdom and Europe by Airlift Book Company.

Library of Congress Cataloging-in-Publication Data
Bannos, Jimmy.
    The Heaven on Seven cookbook : Where it's Mardi Gras all the time! / by Jimmy Bannos and John DeMers.
       p.   cm.
    ISBN 1-58008-168-1
    1. Cookery, American — Louisiana style. 2. Cookery, Cajun 3. Cookery, Creole. I.DeMers, John, 1952- II. Title.
    TX715.2.L68 B36 2001
    641.59763 — dc21   00-057732

Printed in China
First printing, 2000
2 3 4 5 6 7 8 9 10 — 05 04 03 02 01

To my mother, Cathie, who was one of the best cooks and the greatest restaurateurs who ever lived. And to my father, Gus, who taught me that passion and drive were life's most important ingredients. Thanks to them, I've never been afraid of a hard day's work. I miss you both very much.

—*Jimmy Bannos*

TABLE *of* CONTENTS

ACKNOWLEDGMENTS

First and foremost, I'd like to thank my rock, the person who makes my life so easy, my best critic and best friend, my wife, Annamarie. My greatest love goes to my children, Jimmy and Anjelica, the joys of my life. The two of you make me so proud.

And of course:

My brother, George—thanks for always being there, from the beginning.

My "adopted brother" and business partner, Bob Vick—thanks for sharing my vision and letting me creolize you.

Chefs Paulie, George, and Adon—thanks for having the same passion I do, since not enough people do anymore.

Timi and my sister-in-law, Patty, on Wabash, my managers Steve, Brad, Christine, and Michael on Rush, Robert and Ryan on Clark—thanks for holding down the fort. All my past and present staff—you guys rock.

My father-in-law, Sam—thanks for endless late-night talks about New Orleans.

My mother-in-law, Angie—thanks for my Italian food connection.

Chefs Scott Harris, Gabriel Viti, and Patrick Concannon—thanks for all the good times and great food ideas.

New Orleans chefs Paul Prudhomme, Emeril Lagasse, Frank Brigtsen, Susan Spicer, Greg and Mary Sonnier, Gerard Maras, Anthony and Gail Uglesich—thanks for changing my food and my life.

All the "food people" of south Louisiana, including Val Savin, the best fish man I know, and Miss Eula at Savoie's, my Cajun second mother—thanks for teaching me so many great tastes.

Dennis Hayes, Lorena Jones, world champion oyster-eater Phil Wood, and Kirsty Melville at Ten Speed Press, and Dave Peattie and Katherine Silver at BookMatters—thanks for embracing my vision and taking my twenty calls a day.

"Miss Joan" Moravek—thanks for making sure this book didn't take four years to write, with energy boosts from your tofu-carrot shakes. Joanie, you're just so organized! To Joanie's other half, Ron—thanks for letting me invade your home.

My newfound friend and co-author, John DeMers—thanks for being my voice of New Orleans. You're simply the greatest!

And thanks mostly to my customers.

INTRODUCTION

Don't say No way! Don't tell me a Greek kid from an Italian neighborhood in Chicago can't take a Jewish delicatessen on the seventh floor of an office building and grow it into one of America's most successful New Orleans restaurants—950 miles from New Orleans. Don't think that story couldn't happen, because it happened to me.

The story of Heaven on Seven, with three locations and lots of room to grow, is not just about one guy in the kitchen—or even about one guy who found what he wanted to cook and eat, like Dorothy in Oz, a long way from his own backyard. Heaven on Seven is about family, as any story starring Greeks is likely to be. It's about hard work. And it's about luck.

As a third-generation restaurateur, I learned from my mom and dad every ten minutes what some kids today don't pick up in four years of culinary school. As for hard work and luck, in the restaurant business they tend to show up at the same table. Success with a restaurant isn't like winning at the track, which happens just because you're holding the right ticket. But success with a restaurant can be like hitting the Trifecta—as long as you remember you have to carry the horse!

My story is different from others you may have heard, even among chefs cooking Louisi-ana food. When I first tasted New Orleans cuisine it grabbed me by the taste buds—and by the heart. I knew then exactly what I had to do and exactly where I had to do it. My dream involved the flavors of New Orleans, plus a thousand other flavors I hadn't tasted or even dreamed of yet, and it involved a city far to the north. The tropical, laid-back, Gulf-breezed voodoo I felt so strongly would turn out to be either a stroke of genius or a really bad joke. Could it actually be Mardi Gras all the time—in the hard-driven Windy City of Carl Sandburg, Richard Daley, and Mike Ditka?

In creating Heaven on Seven, I was counting on the Chicago I knew and loved to live up to its press releases. And I was counting on the America that beckoned my ancestors to make good on its larger-than-life plateful of promises.

The Little Coffeeshop That Could

Growing up in a big, strong-hearted, pushy town like Chicago, you quickly learn who's who and what's what; you almost suck it out of the water supply. And you figure out where and how you fit in.

Everything's easier if you have a good family, one that becomes a kind of small town for you when you need some R&R. One of the reasons Greeks have done so well in Chicago is that we have at least two small towns to run to whenever the city gets too big—we have our families, which are as extended as they come, and we have the small town of all other Greeks.

Still, while the old folks would have laughed at a word like "diversity," living in a microcosm also taught you there was more to this world than your small piece of it. There was weird and wonderful stuff across the street, stuff you'd never seen or heard of, smelled, or tasted. I figured this out along the way. From an early age, I tried just about any food that didn't try me first.

When the time came, I married none of the Greek girls my grandparents would have picked out, but a lovely Italian

named Annamarie. In making that one decision, I gave my future children bloodlines from the two most excitable cultures on earth. And things are never boring around our house.

At one time I thought about doing something other than cooking for a living—maybe being a veterinarian—but that notion didn't last long. You see, not only my mother and father were in the restaurant business, but so were both sets of my grandparents, not to mention uncles and cousins who worked in the restaurants, cafes, and diners my family operated over the years.

My ancestors came to America from the rock-hard interior of Greece, my father's father making his way here to build the railroad from Chicago to San Francisco. After that job, he settled in Chicago and took a bride in an arranged marriage—one of those Old Country traditions that lasted, for a while at least, in the New Country. Together they ran a diner in one of the city's rail yards. And when my grandfather retired, his two brothers and my grandmother bought a restaurant together.

On my mother's side of the family, my grandfather had a diner in Cicero, Illinois, which during the 1920s and 1930s was quite an exotic place. It was Al Capone's crime headquarters during and after the wild days of Prohibition. My grandmother on this side awakened the chef within me: she filled her house with the smells of baking bread, simmering avgolemono soup, and roasting chicken with oregano. On busy days at the restaurant, I slept over at my grandmother's so my mother could work. There I was baptized into the business as a two-year-old, playing with pots and pans on the floor at my grandmother's feet. The restaurant business was in my blood.

After that, I think my Dad had the most to do with who and how I am in my restaurants today. He was an ex-Marine, and he acted the part in his kitchen, God help us. In the 1960s he ran a steakhouse with a discipline that applied to himself and to everyone who worked for him. I got my work ethic from him, along with my understanding of the simple transaction at the heart of the restaurant business. You buy $100 worth of ingredients. You use $100 worth of ingredients. You keep whatever money is left. Simple! Underlying that simple transaction is the work ethic: everything you do had better be honest, and nothing comes from nothing.

By the time I turned nine, I was working with my brother George in my dad's restaurant; my mother came in to help on Fridays. My dad was the chef — roasting pork, saucing meatloaf, whipping up fried perch and macaroni. There was never any downtime in a restaurant, he taught me. If I wasn't washing dishes, I was peeling potatoes. If I wasn't peeling potatoes, I was sweeping the floor. Today, at Heaven on Seven, I see young people standing around between mealtimes, laughing and looking at their watches. Obviously, they never worked for my dad.

By my junior year in high school, I knew restauranting was for me. I was already working at my dad's in the summer from 5 A.M. till 3 P.M., but I was also hawking cigars, maps, and other things for cash at the La Salle train station. For a high school kid, I was pulling down serious money.

Because I wanted to earn more, though, and to broaden my opportunities in the restaurant business, I went to chef school at a place called Washburne Trade School. I cajoled my parents into sending me, arguing that I needed to be ready for those nights when the chef quit right in the middle of service. Every restaurant has

such nights, so they didn't take much convincing.

Though school and its various internships were hard (I had to quit the three softball teams) they directed my career path toward cooking that was more complex than any my family had ever done. I never stopped loving the simple traditional dishes, the clichés that everybody's mom used to make with love; yet under the critical eye of a French chef named Guy Petite, I honed my techniques for a thousand classics I'd only read about till then.

I even began using what I learned at chef school in my family's restaurant, but the lease ran out before I could really make my mark. My dad thought we should take a year off, to let the family decide what to get into next. I spent my "year off" as chef in an Italian restaurant right in the Loop of downtown Chicago. The money was good, I almost never worked nights, and I was able to have some kind of social life again. It didn't last very long.

My family found the Garland Coffeeshop on the seventh floor of a narrow, high-rise office building of the same name. That space on Wabash Avenue was a Jewish delicatessen owned by a man and his son-in-law who wanted out. We bought the place in December 1979 and opened for business in February. Though we'd all worked through the holidays to get ready, we were cleaning and painting for months.

For me as a trained chef, leaving the Italian restaurant was a major sacrifice. I took a huge cut in salary and worked almost round-the-clock. But I had little choice but to be there for the people who had always been there for me. Perhaps to console myself, I started veering with a vengeance from the old deli's reliance on canned and frozen items, insisting upon fresh produce and from-scratch preparation. I did my own butchering, which was pretty extreme for a coffeeshop; but the effort paid off in customer response. I cooked Italian or Greek or American as the spirit moved me. For years, our Reuben sandwich was voted the best in all of Chicago—a city with a lot of Reubens.

Then, in the mid-1980s, something happened that changed my cooking and, by extension, my life. I picked up a cookbook by a Louisiana chef named Paul Prudhomme. I basked in its peculiar yet vivid interactions with that region's Cajun and Creole cuisines. And I, a Greek kid cooking in the Loop of Chicago, vowed to try some of those dishes in our coffeeshop.

I'd never even visited New Orleans, but something about that city's cooking intrigued me. I read everything I could. I quizzed everybody I met who'd been there, including my father-in-law, whose pecan business regularly carried him south. And when it seemed I couldn't postpone the pilgrimage any longer, I picked up the telephone and dialed the number of New Orleans chef par excellence Paul Prudhomme.

All these years later, I suppose that if Chef Paul had been rude or impatient with me, my whole story might have taken a different turn. But he was warm and welcoming and passionate about everybody's food, and especially Creole and Cajun. Paul encouraged me to meet him when I came to New Orleans. So off I went with my wife. I found K-Paul's in the French Quarter. And I sat at the small table by the kitchen where the master evaluated everything his cook put out. Our conversation evolved into a night in K-Paul's kitchen, where I experienced a whole new type of food, developed a new love, and began a new way of living.

The place was electric. Frank Brigtsen, Greg and Mary Sonnier, and other chefs who have since opened restaurants of their own, jammed to put out great food. They talked about each dish and each technique, and also told me about other people I needed to meet—Gerard Maras, then at Mr. B's; Emeril Lagasse, then at Commander's Palace. I felt the doors opening for me, not just to the dining rooms but also to the kitchens of chefs who would become my mentors, my heroes, and my friends. Through their eyes, New Orleans became real for me: a spectacular new world of music, attitude, and best of all, unbelievable food.

Traveling to New Orleans became a regular part of life for me and Annamarie. We ate countless meals in palaces like Commander's and Galatoire's as well as in beloved dives like Central Grocery (known for its muffalettas) and Uglesich's (famous for Gulf oysters). It wasn't long before the Garland Coffeeshop began to reflect our infatuation. We offered specials such as gumbo and red beans and crawfish—and as people came to love and request them, we had to begin making them every day. This was a big deal for Chicago, where if people used crawfish for anything it was for bait.

In 1985, right before Lent, I pulled together about ten of these specials, decorated the whole place in purple, green, and gold, and called it (what else?) Mardi Gras. The newspaper covered the event, as did one or more TV stations. Suddenly, for a place on the seventh floor with no sign on the street, the New Garland Coffeeshop had become a destination restaurant. You might think we had arrived—except that in the restaurant business, every time you get someplace there's someplace new you have to go.

I may have needed an epiphany—and I got one. One day in the shower (really!), I was thinking about the design for a T-shirt I was trying to produce. I kept picturing a big bowl of gumbo with steam rising. Rising where? To heaven, of course. Heaven rhymed with seven. Hmm… For many, our place was already a little bit of heaven on seven. Before long, Heaven on Seven it was.

Business was good on Wabash. There were women who came in for breakfast every day, compassionate, fun-loving people. They were almost our sales force. The building also had

about eighty psychiatrists. They treated us like bartenders, coming in after a hard day at the office for advice about life and love—from us!

Once I began cooking New Orleans, I could justify more trips there, sometimes with my wife, sometimes with my brother George. Each weekend crash course might feature as many as twenty-five restaurants. We drafted an elderly cab driver named Robert into our entourage, to help us get from restaurant to restaurant. Sometimes we had a different course at each one; sometimes we stayed in one place, tasting dish after dish, then telling the server to box up the leftovers. Robert loved to see us hit town. In addition to the fare, his family and friends ate well for days after one of our weekends.

As our customers grew in number, with long but happy lines at lunch, it became impossible for me not to think about expanding. Whatever we called it, our place on Wabash was still a coffeeshop at heart. It had 120 seats in just 1,700 square feet. And the kitchen takes up very few of those feet. For its part, Chicago was taking off, especially tourism near the shopping on Michigan Avenue. Wabash would remain Wabash—we even started opening for dinner the first and third Fridays of each month—but Heaven

on Seven needed to take some giant steps onto what Chicago calls the Magnificent Mile.

So we opened a second Heaven on Seven on Rush Street. This location across from the Disney Quest attraction has 160 seats—but a full 4,200 square feet to accommodate the people sitting in them. That means we also get a real kitchen, and most of the cooking takes place right in front of customers at our long, friendly, often-frenzied food bar. There's enough room for prep work, dishwashing, and even a couple of offices in the back. The walls are a gallery for my signature collection of hot pepper sauces from all over the world. Wabash has 10 employees, Rush Street about 100. Every day, in the big restaurant, I come up with ten or twelve specials. Some folks come in and say "Jimmy, feed me"—they get a multicourse tasting orgy. I especially like it when "feed me" customers and people at other tables who've ordered, say, simple fried oyster po-boys, get into excited conversations about their food.

My third Heaven on Seven on Clark Street near Wrigley Field is exciting in several ways. For starters, this location is my first on the ground floor—and nearly all restaurants in New Orleans are on the ground floor. A thousand touches—from plantation shutters to French doors opening onto the patio, from moss-green colors to slow-turning fans—my vision of New Orleans can be more real than ever.

It's my job, I think, to infect people with my passion, starting with my staff. I'm from the school where everything comes from the top—with my father, how could I have turned out any other way? If something doesn't happen right in the kitchen or in the dining room, the only one I ever really blame is me.

This business never stops. It never gets boring. And it never ceases to surprise me—with the good, the bad, and sometimes the ugly. You have to love it. But by this time you've figured out that I really do!

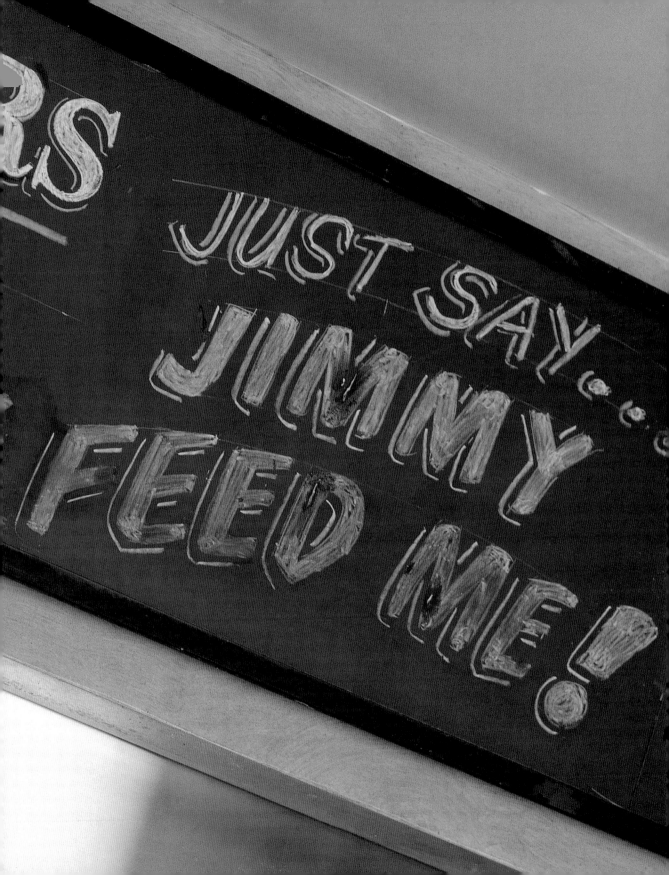

Jimmy's Kitchen

My kitchen and the pantry that keeps it cooking are crazy, mixed-up, wonderful places. Because so much of my food is inspired by the Creole and Cajun cuisines I've tasted in New Orleans, there's always room for the latest ingredient I've discovered there—beginning with the andouille, tasso, and Gulf seafoods that are that city's stock in trade. Still, in this new century I feel as free as most chefs do these days to borrow over the back fence of the world.

If I think an ingredient from Asia would work in a dish I want to cook, an ingredient from Asia should feel right at home. The same goes for a pepper from Latin America or a tropical fruit from the Caribbean. I love the fact that so many doors are open now—for fresh products and fresh ideas—and the fact that so many chefs know what to do with an open door.

The following ingredients all turn up often in my cooking. Feel free to learn from me whatever strikes your fancy, but follow your own taste buds when they take you in a different direction. After all, if I hadn't followed my taste buds to some pretty unexpected places, I wouldn't be doing what I'm doing now.

Andouille

It drives me crazy when recipes from Louisiana call for andouille "or Polish kielbasa." I grew up in a city with a Little Warsaw, so I know kielbasa—and good as it can be, one thing it ain't is andouille. Andouille is a Cajun smoked-pork sausage, often with a bite from hot pepper. The stuff is wonderful, whether sliced open and grilled for a po-boy or cut into coins or chunks and added to gumbo. You'll love the smoky tang it gives to just about anything it touches. Andouille is sold nationwide in some stores and meat markets, and several Louisiana companies also offer it mail order.

Greens

There was a time, I'm told, that greens were eaten only by the "have-nots" in society—which of course meant that the "haves" were missing out. Now, everybody knows greens are terrific. And they're even relatively good for you, if you don't go overboard with the soul-food treatment and cook them in tons of bacon drippings (they do taste good that way, though). Mustard, turnip, and collard greens are among my favorites, and collards are my pick among those.

Hot Peppers

Make no mistake: I like it hot. I'm one of those people (only some of whom are chefs) who never get tired of finding new ways of giving food a kick. When I first started studying Louisiana cooking, that meant adding ground red pepper—the stuff many older cookbooks call simply "cayenne," after the type of pepper from which it was made—or pouring on the hot sauce. Now, however, there's an embarrassment of riches in the hot section of your market. There are fresh jalapeños and habaneros, the second probably being the hottest pepper on earth. There's a virtual designer collection of peppers from the Southwest, from fresh-picked to roasted to dried, each with a different story to tell in your mouth. And there are some tiny-but-deadly hot Asian peppers as well, a regular part of Thai cooking. I guess I've used them all at one time or another, and you should try them all too.

Hot Sauces

If you've looked at the walls of my restaurants, you know I'm a hot sauce fanatic. People bring me hot sauces from their travels, and I'm pretty quick to try them, use them, and at least put them on display. These bottles large and small, red and green, foreign and domestic, are quite a hit with customers, who turn out in droves for my "Hot as a Mutha" dinners—full tasting menus for people who like mouth burn. In this country, the hot sauce biz began with Tabasco from Louisiana's Avery Island about 150 years ago. Tabasco still makes terrific sauce—the traditional red as well as several newer varieties, including a good green jalapeño. Even in Louisiana now, there are pepper sauces galore. My only advice is to find the one that tastes best to you.

Pickled Pork

I like pickled pork beacuse it has great flavor to give bean dishes, jambalayas, and etouffées. In Louisiana, it's often called "salt meat"—but it's not too salty. If you can't get pickled pork, you can use smoked boneless pork shoulder butt.

Seafoods

Like a lot of the world's best cuisines, New Orleans food takes every advantage of its location on the water, with the Gulf of Mexico as well as numerous bays, lakes, and bayous to scour for edibles. The Big Four of Creole and Cajun are finfish, shrimp, oysters, and crabmeat. I mean, the people of New Orleans ought to be ashamed of themselves, hoarding so many of the world's great ingredients in one not-very-big city. And if that weren't enough, something is always coming into season just as something else is going out. The result is a continuous cycle of changing recipes—there's always something great on the menu right now and something else worth looking forward to.

Seasoning Mixes

Of course, my favorite seasoning mix is the one I make. But the fact is that ever since Cajun became cool in the 1980s, Creole and Cajun seasonings have been a standard part of supermarkets nationwide. Each blend varies, but the mainstays in the mix seem to be salt (of course), ground black, red, and white pepper (since each flirts with a different part of your mouth), and garlic. My recipes specify which seasoning mix to use, but feel free to use your own favorite. Most things really do taste better with a shake or three of Louisiana seasoning, whatever the recipe.

Sweet Potatoes

You can't cook anything with sweet potatoes without adding the subtitle "Out of Africa," for this bright orange, sweet-tasting starch has the continent written all over it. In Louisiana, with its rich heritage of interaction between French-speaking whites and French-speaking blacks, sweet potatoes are something both races can accurately claim as their mama's cooking.

Tasso Ham

Here's another of those Louisiana products that just doesn't have a substitute. It's a very smoky, very salty Cajun ham, used far more often as a seasoning than as a meat. You wouldn't, for instance, bite into a tasso and cheese sandwich. But if you wanted to shave off a few slivers and use it for punch in a cream reduction sauce being served over pasta, most folks in Louisiana would say, "Now you're talking!"

Tomatoes

We're pretty sure tomatoes showed up in Louisiana cuisine during the brief and corrupt rule of the Spanish, who offered the colony a change from the long and corrupt rule of the French. The word *Creole* (or *criollo*, originally) hinted at dishes of Spanish origin. Today, as we see in shrimp Creole, it means anything cooked in or covered with one of those red tomato sauces given interest by chopped onion, green pepper, and celery—the mix often called the Holy Trinity by New Orleans cooks. Since New Orleans is a fairly religious town (by its own lights!), it's a safe bet the nickname is not sacrilegious.

APPETIZERS

CRAB CAKES
WITH HONEY-JALAPEÑO DRESSING ~ 14

BAYOU CAKES WITH HOT REMOULADE SAUCE ~ 16

MUFFALETTA CALZONE ~ 18

ANGRY MUSSELS ~ 19

SHRIMP AND ANDOUILLE EGG ROLLS
WITH GINGERED MANGO SAUCE ~ 20

JERK CHICKEN WINGS WITH HABANERO
CHILE—MANGO SAUCE ~ 22

RED HOT CHILE—RUBBED PORK SKEWERS
WITH CILANTRO-CUCUMBER TZATZIKI SAUCE ~ 23

PARMESAN-CRUSTED CRAWFISH-STUFFED SHIITAKE
(WITH AVERY ISLAND SAUCE) ~ 24

GRILLED SEA SCALLOPS AND PINEAPPLE OVER
ARUGULA WITH PINEAPPLE-LIME VINAIGRETTE ~ 28

TOMATO STACK
WITH HERB-CRUSTED GOAT CHEESE ~ 29

CREOLE CAESAR SALAD
WITH CREOLE CAESAR DRESSING ~ 30

NEW ORLEANS COBB SALAD
WITH PAULIE'S BLUE-CHEESE DRESSING ~ 31

Crab Cakes with Honey-Jalapeño Dressing

Makes 18 cakes; serves 6

I love almost any combination of hot and sweet, and here's a dish that says it all in that department. Though it won't burn your mouth off, you can definitely taste the cayenne and jalapeño, which are nicely balanced by the sweetness of honey. Best of all, you can use this dressing on a whole bunch of things, from salads to fried catfish to po-boys.

Honey-Jalapeño Dressing

⅔ cup mayonnaise
½ cup heavy whipping cream
⅓ cup thinly sliced green onion, white and green parts
1½ teaspoons seeded and minced jalapeño
4 teaspoons honey
¼ teaspoon Worcestershire sauce
¼ teaspoon hot pepper sauce
⅛ teaspoon freshly ground black pepper
⅛ teaspoon ground white pepper
⅛ teaspoon ground cayenne

Crab Cake Mixture

¼ cup unsalted butter
1½ cups seeded, finely diced green bell pepper
½ cup finely diced celery
2 tablespoons thinly sliced green onion, white and green parts
2 tablespoons minced red onion
2 tablespoons minced yellow onion
1 tablespoon seeded and minced jalapeño
2 teaspoons Roasted-Garlic Purée (page 142)
2 teaspoons Creole mustard
1 teaspoon Worcestershire sauce
½ teaspoon hot pepper sauce

2 teaspoons Angel Dust Cajun Seasoning (page 137)
⅛ teaspoon freshly ground black pepper
⅛ teaspoon ground white pepper
⅛ teaspoon crushed red pepper flakes
1 pound rock crabmeat or blue crabmeat, drained and picked through for shells
1⅛ cup dried bread crumbs
¼ cup grated Asiago cheese, preferably medium-aged
1 tablespoon minced fresh parsley
1 large egg
1 tablespoon water
¼ teaspoon Angel Dust Cajun Seasoning (page 137)
¾ cup Japanese Bread Crumbs (page 136)
Vegetable oil for frying

To prepare the dressing, whisk the mayonnaise and cream together in a medium-sized bowl. Add the remaining ingredients. Cover and refrigerate until ready to serve.

To prepare the crab cakes, melt the butter in a large nonstick sauté pan over medium-high heat. Add the bell pepper, celery, onions, jalapeño, and garlic purée and sauté for 5 minutes until softened. Reduce the heat to medium and add the mustard, Worcestershire and hot pepper sauces, and the seasonings; cook for an additional 10 minutes. Add the crabmeat and heat through for 1 minute. Transfer the mixture to a large bowl and mix in the bread crumbs, cheese, and parsley. Cover with plastic wrap and chill in the refrigerator for 1 hour.

Form the chilled mixture into 18 small ½-inch-thick cakes. In one pie plate, beat together the eggs, water, and Cajun seasoning in one; place the seasoned breadcrumb mixture in another pie plate. Coat each crab cake with the egg, then with the bread crumbs, and transfer to a cookie sheet.

Heat 2½ inches of vegetable oil to 350° in a heavy 4-quart saucepan. Fry cakes in small batches until golden brown, 1½ to 2 minutes per batch. Drain on paper towels. Keep warm in a 200° oven until all cakes are fried.

Serve 3 crab cakes per person along with the honey-jalapeño dressing.

BAYOU CAKES WITH HOT REMOULADE SAUCE

MAKES 18 CAKES; SERVES 6

This satisfying dish folds crawfish and shrimp into my basic crab cakes—a kind of southern Louisiana hat trick. The pungent remoulade is given bite with grainy Creole mustard. I break with tradition by smoothing the sauce with cream rather than emulsifying it with oil.

Hot Remoulade Sauce

- ¼ cup ketchup
- ¼ cup diced celery
- 2 tablespoons chopped fresh parsley
- 1 tablespoon sliced green onion, white and green parts
- 1 tablespoon water
- 2 teaspoons prepared horseradish
- 2 teaspoons Creole mustard
- 1 teaspoon yellow mustard
- 1 teaspoon freshly squeezed lemon juice
- 1 teaspoon Roasted-Garlic Pureé (page 142)
- 1 cup heavy whipping cream
- ½ teaspoon Hungarian paprika
- ½ teaspoon Spanish paprika
- ¼ teaspoon chile powder
- ½ teaspoon Angel Dust Cajun Seasoning (page 137)
- ⅛ teaspoon freshly ground black pepper
- ⅛ teaspoon ground white pepper
- ⅛ teaspoon crushed red pepper flakes
- ⅛ teaspoon Worcestershire sauce
- ⅛ teaspoon hot pepper sauce
- ½ teaspoon cornstarch mixed with ½ teaspoon water
- 1 tablespoon unsalted butter, chilled and cut into pieces

Bayou Cake Mixture

- ½ recipe Crab Cake Mixture (page 14)
- 5 ounces rock shrimp or small shrimp, peeled and deveined
- 5 ounces crawfish tail meat, rinsed, drained, and coarsely chopped
- 2 tablespoons grated Asiago cheese, preferably medium-aged
- ½ teaspoon Worcestershire sauce
- ½ teaspoon hot pepper sauce
- ½ teaspoon Angel Dust Cajun Seasoning (page 137)
- 1 large egg
- 1 tablespoon water
- ¼ teaspoon Angel Dust Cajun Seasoning (page 137)
- ¾ cup Japanese Bread Crumbs (page 136)
- Vegetable oil for frying

To prepare the remoulade sauce, purée the ketchup, celery, parsley, green onion, water, horseradish, mustards, lemon juice, and garlic purée in a blender until smooth. In a medium saucepan, combine the purée with the cream, paprikas, chili powder, and Cajun seasoning. Bring the mixture to a boil over high heat and cook for 5 minutes, whisking continuously. Decrease the heat to medium-low, add the black and white peppers, red pepper flakes, Worcestershire and hot pepper sauces, and continue cooking for an additional 5 minutes.

Whisk in the cornstarch mixture and heat the sauce over low heat for 1 minute, until it thickens, then whisk in the butter a little at a time. Remove from the heat until needed. Rewarm before serving.

Prepare the crab cake mixture. Bring a small pot of water to a boil, add the shrimp, and simmer for 1 to 1½ minutes, until the shrimp are no longer translucent. Drain, coarsely chop, and transfer to a bowl along with the crab cake mixture. Add crawfish tail meat, cheese, Worcestershire and hot pepper sauces, and Cajun seasoning to the crab and shrimp mixture, and combine thoroughly. Cover with plastic wrap and chill in the refrigerator for 1 hour.

Form the chilled mixture into 18 small ½-inch-thick cakes. In one pie plate, beat together the egg, water, and Cajun seasoning; place the seasoned bread crumb mixture in another. Coat each bayou cake with the egg, then with the bread crumbs, and transfer to a cookie sheet.

Heat 2½ inches of vegetable oil to 350° in a heavy 4-quart saucepan. Fry cakes in small batches until golden brown, 1½ to 2 minutes per batch. Drain on paper towels. Keep warm in a 200° oven until all cakes are fried.

Serve 3 bayou cakes per person along with the hot remoulade sauce.

MUFFALETTA CALZONE

A great Sicilian sandwich based on the flavors of New Orleans was an idea whose time had to come. I'm just happy to be the guy who made it happen. We fill the calzone dough with all the Italian cold cuts and cheese that would go on the sandwich, bake it till the cheese is molten, then spoon garlicky olive salad over the outside. Next time, you'll want this for dinner instead of pizza.

Calzone Dough

- 1 cup warm water (110° to 115°)
- 1 package active dry yeast
- Pinch of sugar
- 2½ cups all-purpose flour, plus additional as needed
- ½ teaspoon salt
- 2 tablespoons olive oil

Filling

- 1 pound provolone cheese, cut into thin strips
- 4 ounces mortadella, cut into thin strips
- 4 ounces Genoa salami, cut into thin strips
- 4 ounces baked ham, cut into thin strips
- 1 large egg, lightly beaten with 2 teaspoons water
- 2⅔ cups Jimmy's Olive Salad (page 92)

To prepare the dough, pour the warm water in a small bowl. Sprinkle the yeast and sugar onto the top of the water. Briefly let the water absorb the yeast, then stir to dissolve it. Let stand for 15 minutes until the mixture is foamy. In the bowl of a heavy-duty electric mixer fitted with the paddle attachment, combine 1½ cups of the flour and the salt on low speed. Add the

yeast mixture and oil, and beat until smooth, about 1 minute. Add the remaining 1 cup of flour and beat for 1 minute, until the dough just clears the sides of the bowl. Turn the dough out on a lightly floured work surface and knead for 2 to 3 minutes, until dough is smooth and elastic. The dough should be soft, but use additional flour as needed, a tablespoon at a time. Place the dough in a lightly oiled bowl, cover with plastic wrap, and allow to rest in a warm place until tripled in bulk, about 1½ hours. Cut the dough into 8 pieces and roll each into a ball. Using a rolling pin or your hand, flatten into 6-inch circles on a lightly floured surface.

Preheat oven to 425°.

To fill the calzones, distribute the cheese and meat equally among the 8 circles of dough, placing the fillings on the lower third of each circle. Moisten the edges of each dough circle with water. Fold the top half of the dough over the bottom half to form a half moon, and seal the edges by crimping with a fork. Lightly brush the top and edges of each calzone with the egg wash.

Place on a baking sheet lined with parchment paper and bake until golden brown, 18 to 20 minutes.

Serve each calzone on top of a small mound of Jimmy's Olive Salad.

ANGRY MUSSELS

Actually, I expect these mussels will make you happy, not angry. I borrowed the name from a sauce I tasted at Uglesich's in New Orleans—the underground-hit, hole-in-the-wall place for oysters a million ways. The name is about all I borrowed, since from there I let the hot peppers tell me what to do. This sauce is hotter than hell but has a great taste. You'll be sweating as you eat it, but if you're like me you won't be able to stop.

Angry Sauce

- 2 tablespoons extra virgin olive oil
- 1 tablespoon unsalted butter
- 1¼ cups diced yellow onion
- 3 tablespoons sliced garlic
- 1 teaspoon Roasted-Garlic Purée (page 142)
- 1½ teaspoons sugar
- ½ teaspoon crushed red pepper flakes
- ¼ teaspoon Angel Dust Cajun Seasoning (page 137)
- ⅛ teaspoon freshly ground black pepper
- ⅛ teaspoon ground white pepper
- ⅛ teaspoon ground habanero chile powder
- 1½ cups diced plum tomatoes
- ⅔ cup water
- 2 tablespoons red chile paste (Sambal Oelek)
- Pinch of salt
- 2 pounds mussels, scrubbed and debearded

In a medium sauté pan, heat the oil and butter over medium heat. Add the onions and cook, stirring frequently, for 15 minutes, until they begin to caramelize but not burn. Turn the heat to low and add the sliced garlic and garlic purée, sugar, red pepper flakes, black and white peppers, and habanero chile powder. Cook for an additional 5 minutes. When the garlic softens and begins to turn golden brown, stir in the tomatoes, water, and chile paste. Bring to a simmer, and cook over medium heat for 10 minutes. Mix in the salt.

Heat the sauce in a Dutch oven and simmer for 2 minutes over high heat. Stir in the mussels and coat them with some of the hot sauce. Cover and decrease the heat to medium. Stir the mussels occasionally and cook for 6 minutes, or until all the shells are open. Discard any mussels that do not open. Divide the mussels and sauce among shallow bowls.

Serve immediately with a crusty white Italian bread.

SHRIMP AND ANDOUILLE EGG ROLLS
with Gingered Mango Sauce

SERVES 8

One of the best ideas to come out of "fusion cuisine" is using different things to fill once-Chinese egg rolls. I love the original, and all I've done here is Creolize it. Then I paired it with a tropical ginger-mango sauce. It's sweet and it's pungent.

Gingered Mango Sauce

  1⅓ cups (1 medium) peeled, chopped
      mango
  1 tablespoon water
  1 teaspoon peeled and grated fresh ginger
  1 teaspoon freshly squeezed lemon juice
  1 teaspoon honey
  Pinch of salt
  Pinch of ground white pepper

Egg Roll Filling

  7 ounces small shrimp, peeled and
      deveined
  1 tablespoon sesame seeds
  5 ounces andouille sausage, sliced
      into ¼-inch slices and chopped
  4 teaspoons sesame oil
  3½ cups finely shredded green cabbage
  ½ cup finely diced celery
  ½ cup thinly sliced green onion, green and
      white parts
  2 teaspoons peeled and minced fresh
      ginger
  1 teaspoon minced garlic
  ½ teaspoon Roasted-Garlic Purée
      (page 142)
  ⅓ cup finely shredded carrots
  1 tablespoon Creole mustard
  ¼ teaspoon Angel Dust Cajun Seasoning
      (page 137)

⅛ teaspoon salt
Pinch of ground white pepper
1 large egg, lightly beaten
Eight (6½ by 6½-inch) egg roll wrappers
Water

To prepare the sauce, purée all ingredients in a blender. Refrigerate until needed.

To cook the shrimp, bring a small pot of water to a boil. Add the shrimp, reduce the heat, and simmer for 1½ minutes. Drain and chop coarsely. Transfer to a large mixing bowl. Set aside.

In a large nonstick sauté pan, toast the sesame seeds over medium-high heat, shaking the pan back and forth so the seeds do not burn. Transfer the seeds to the bowl containing the shrimp.

In the same pan, sauté the andouille over medium-high heat for 4 minutes to render the fat. Drain the andouille on paper towels, then transfer the sausage to the mixing bowl. With a paper towel, wipe the pan of any remaining fat from the andouille. Heat the pan over medium-high heat, add the sesame oil, and sauté the cabbage, celery, onions, ginger, garlic, and garlic purée for 3 minutes. Stir in the carrots, mustard, Cajun seasoning, salt, and pepper and heat through for 1 minute. Transfer the vegetable mixture to the bowl. Cool in the refrigerator for 15 minutes, then fold in the beaten egg.

Lay an egg roll wrapper on the work surface with one of the corners facing downward. Place

½ cup of the mixture on the lower third of the wrapper. To roll, begin by turning the lower corner halfway up over the filling. Lightly moisten the exposed edges of the wrapper with water. Fold the two side corners inward over the filling and continue to roll up. Press the top corner firmly onto the egg roll to seal it. Repeat for each egg roll. Fry immediately.

Heat 2½ inches of vegetable oil to 350° in a heavy 4-quart saucepan. Fry 3 or 4 egg rolls at a time until golden brown, about 4 minutes per batch. Keep warm in a 200° oven until all egg rolls are fried.

Serve with the gingered-mango sauce.

Note
This recipe could easily be doubled and frozen for future use. Uncooked egg rolls should be lightly dusted with cornstarch, individually wrapped, then placed in a plastic freezer bag and immediately frozen.

JERK CHICKEN WINGS
with Habanero Chile–Mango Sauce

SERVES 6

Eat your heart out, Buffalo. If folks want hot wings, they know Jamaica is a better place to go shopping than upstate New York. For this one, I kick the chicken with both my wet jerk marinade and my dry jerk rub. Just try to tell me you don't get the island flavor!

Habanero Chile–Mango Sauce

    1 teaspoon extra virgin olive oil
    ¼ cup diced yellow onion
    ½ teaspoon seeded, chopped habanero
        chile
    ¼ teaspoon Roasted-Garlic Purée
        (page 142)
    1⅓ cups (1 medium) peeled, chopped
        mango
    2 tablespoons water
    1 teaspoon honey
    Pinch of salt
    Pinch of ground white pepper
    2 tablespoons minced fresh cilantro
    3 pounds chicken wings, rinsed and
        patted dry
    1 tablespoon plus ½ teaspoon Dry Rub
        Jerk Seasoning (page 137)
    ½ cup Jimmy's Jamaican Jerk Marinade
        (page 138)
    ½ teaspoon Angel Dust Cajun Seasoning
        (page 137)
    Nonstick vegetable spray

To prepare the chile-mango sauce, heat the oil over high heat in a small nonstick sauté pan. Add the onions and cook, stirring frequently, for 1 minute. Add the chile and garlic purée and cook for an additional minute. Transfer the mixture to a blender along with the mango, water, honey, salt, and pepper, and purée until smooth. Pour the sauce into a small container, stir in the cilantro, cover, and refrigerate for at least 30 minutes before serving, or overnight until needed.

To prepare the wings, remove the wing tip at the first joint and discard or reserve for another use, such as making chicken stock. Cut the remaining portion into two sections by cutting through the joint. Each wing will yield two pieces.

Season the chicken wings with 1 tablespoon of the jerk seasoning. Place the chicken in a plastic resealable bag and add the jerk marinade, coating all the pieces evenly. Seal the bag and marinate in the refrigerator for at least 8 hours and up to 24 hours.

When ready to cook, preheat the oven to 375°. Line a baking sheet with aluminum foil and spray with the nonstick vegetable spray. Remove the chicken wings from the plastic bag and transfer to the prepared pan. Discard the the marinade. Combine the remaining ½ teaspoon of jerk seasoning with the Cajun seasoning and sprinkle both sides of the wings with the mixture. Bake for 25 minutes; then turn the chicken wings over and bake for 15 more minutes, until the marinade on the wings begins to brown.

Serve with the chile-mango sauce.

Red Hot Chile–Rubbed Pork Skewers
with Cilantro-Cucumber Tzatziki Sauce

SERVES 6

I get a kind of secret thrill every time I find a great place to celebrate my Greek heritage in food. This dish reminds me of street foods I sampled as a kid visiting Greece; I have spiced it up a bit and substituted cilantro for mint.

Cilantro-Cucumber Tzatziki Sauce
1 cup plain yogurt, preferably whole-milk
¼ cup finely diced, seeded cucumber
1 tablespoon minced fresh cilantro
1 tablespoon freshly squeezed lime juice
1 teaspoon minced garlic
½ teaspoon kosher salt
⅛ teaspoon ground white pepper

Red Hot Chile Marinade
½ teaspoon ground chile de Árbol powder
½ teaspoon ground ancho chile powder
½ teaspoon ground cayenne
½ teaspoon ground cumin
⅓ cup freshly squeezed orange juice
2 tablespoons water
1 teaspoon Roasted-Garlic Purée (page 142)
½ teaspoon cane syrup or light molasses
½ teaspoon ground Mexican oregano
3 tablespoons extra virgin olive oil
1½ pounds trimmed pork tenderloin
1 teaspoon plus ½ teaspoon Angel Dust Cajun Seasoning (page 137)
1 teaspoon Dry Rub Jerk Seasoning (page 137)
¼ teaspoon salt
¼ teaspoon freshly ground black pepper
⅛ teaspoon ground chile de Arbol powder
2 teaspoons extra virgin olive oil
Skewers (if wooden, soaked in water)

To make the sauce, whisk all the ingredients together in a small bowl. Cover and refrigerate until needed.

To make the marinade, heat the chile de Arbol powder, ancho chile powder, cayenne, and cumin for 45 to 60 seconds in a small sauté pan over medium-low heat. Transfer the spice mixture to a small bowl, and whisk in the orange juice, water, garlic purée, cane syrup, and oregano. Gradually whisk in the oil in a steady stream.

Season the meat with 1 teaspoon of the Cajun seasoning and the jerk seasoning. Place pork into a plastic resealable bag, add the marinade, and seal the bag. Marinate in the refrigerator for at least 8 hours and up to 24 hours.

When ready to cook, heat a charcoal or gas grill. Remove the pork from the plastic bag and discard the marinade. Slice the tenderloin into 12 equal portions. Working with one piece at a time, place a piece of pork between two pieces of plastic wrap and pound out to a thickness of ⅛ inch. Complete with remaining tenderloin pieces. Combine the remaining ½ teaspoon Cajun seasoning with the salt, pepper, and chile de Arbol powder. Lightly brush both sides of the meat with the olive oil and sprinkle with the seasoning mixture. Thread each piece of pork onto a skewer (for stability, use two skewers for each piece of meat). Grill over medium-high heat for 6 to 7 minutes, turning occasionally.

Serve immediately with the sauce.

PARMESAN-CRUSTED CRAWFISH-STUFFED SHIITAKE
with *Avery Island Sauce*

SERVES 6

*Down in New Orleans, they seem to stuff every-
thing they can get their hands on with crabmeat.
Here I blend the crab with cheese for texture, then
press the whole business into a full-flavored shiitake
mushroom, or maybe a portobello. Some mushroom
with punch. For the Avery Island Sauce (named
after the southern Louisiana home of Tabasco),
I combine that wonderful hot pepper sauce with
my own Heavenly Blend (you can order this from
heavenonseven.com). The brown sugar adds that
special touch of sweetness that I like.*

Avery Island Sauce
4 teaspoons extra virgin olive oil
⅓ cup finely diced yellow onion
1 teaspoon Roasted-Garlic Purée (page 142)
½ teaspoon Tabasco sauce
2 cups (about 4 medium) diced plum
  tomatoes
2 (5.5-ounce) cans tomato juice
1½ cups water
½ teaspoon hot pepper sauce
1 tablespoon dark brown sugar
1 tablespoon light brown sugar
1 tablespoon granulated sugar
⅛ teaspoon Angel Dust Cajun Seasoning
  (page 137)
⅛ teaspoon ground jalapeño powder
⅛ teaspoon freshly ground black pepper
⅛ teaspoon ground white pepper
⅛ teaspoon crushed red pepper flakes
⅛ teaspoon kosher salt

Crawfish Filling
2 tablespoons unsalted butter
½ cup finely diced celery

1 cup seeded, finely diced green
  bell pepper
¼ cup thinly sliced green onion, white
  and green parts
1½ tablespoons minced red onion
1½ tablespoons minced yellow onion
1 tablespoon seeded and minced jalapeño
2 teaspoons Roasted-Garlic Purée
  (page 142)
2 teaspoons Creole mustard
1 teaspoon Worcestershire sauce
½ teaspoon hot pepper sauce
1½ teaspoons Angel Dust Cajun
  Seasoning (page 137)
⅛ teaspoon freshly ground black pepper
⅛ teaspoon ground white pepper
⅛ teaspoon crushed red pepper flakes

12 ounces crawfish tail meat, rinsed,
  drained, and coarsely chopped
⅓ cup dried bread crumbs
⅓ cup grated Asiago cheese, preferably
  medium-aged
1 tablespoon minced fresh parsley
18 large shiitake mushrooms,
  stems removed
2 tablespoons Garlic Oil (page 142)
1 teaspoon Angel Dust Cajun Seasoning
  (page 137)
½ cup grated Parmesan cheese

To make the Avery Island Sauce, heat the oil
in a 2-quart saucepan over medium-high heat.
Add the onion and sauté for 5 minutes, stirring
frequently. Add the garlic purée and Tabasco
sauce and continue cooking for 3 minutes. Stir
as often as necessary to prevent onions from
burning. Mix in the tomatoes, tomato juice,

water, and hot pepper sauce. Bring to a simmer, reduce the heat to medium, and cook for 5 minutes. Stir in the dark and light brown sugars, granulated sugar, Cajun seasoning, jalapeño powder, ground black and white peppers, red pepper flakes, and salt, and simmer for 25 minutes until the tomatoes begin to break down and sauce thickens. Transfer the sauce to a blender and cover it with the lid. (To prevent any hot liquid from splashing out of the blender, cover the lid with a folded dish towel.) On low speed, pulse on and off several times. Purée the sauce until it is almost smooth but still has some texture from the onions and tomato pulp. Set aside. Reheat before serving.

To prepare the crawfish filling, melt the butter in a large nonstick sauté pan over medium-high heat. Add the bell pepper, celery, onions, jalapeño, and garlic purée and cook until softened, about 5 minutes. Reduce the heat to medium and add the mustard, Worcestershire and hot pepper sauces, and the seasonings. Cook for an additional 8 minutes. Add the crawfish tail meat and heat through for 2 minutes. Transfer the mixture to a large bowl and thoroughly mix in the bread crumbs, cheese, and parsley. Set aside.

Preheat the broiler. Cover a broiler pan or line a heavy jelly roll pan with aluminum foil. Wipe the mushrooms with a damp paper towel. Over medium-high heat, heat the large nonstick sauté pan used to prepare the crawfish filling. Add the garlic olive oil and heat until the oil is hot but not smoking, about 1 minute. Place the mushrooms in a single layer in the sauté pan and sprinkle with ½ teaspoon of Cajun seasoning. With a pair of tongs, turn mushroom caps over and sprinkle with the remaining ½ teaspoon of Cajun seasoning. Continue cooking for 2 minutes, turning once or twice until the mushrooms are cooked through but still retain their shape. Transfer the mushrooms to the foil-lined pan. Divide the crawfish mixture among the caps, pressing the filling down lightly. Sprinkle each mound of filling with Parmesan cheese, pressing lightly so the cheese adheres to the filling. Place the broiler pan or jelly roll pan at least 6 or 7 inches from the heat source. Broil until Parmesan cheese is golden brown, 1 to 1½ minutes, rotating the pan midway through if necessary to ensure even browning.

Serve immediately with warm Avery Island Sauce.

Note
The mushroom caps will burn if they are placed too close to the broiler flame. Be sure they are at least 6 or 7 inches away from the heat source.

GRILLED SEA SCALLOPS AND PINEAPPLE
over Arugula with Pineapple-Lime Vinaigrette

SERVES 4

Scallops provide a refreshing change from shrimp in your salad. Besides, I think scallops and pineapple were made for each other. Try this one in the summer, or whenever you feel like pretending it's summer.

Pineapple-Lime Vinaigrette
  1 cup pineapple juice
  1 tablespoon freshly squeezed lime juice
  1 tablespoon diced red onion
  1 teaspoon honey
  ½ teaspoon Creole mustard
  ½ teaspoon ground ancho chile powder
  ¼ teaspoon Roasted-Garlic Purée
    (page 142)
  ½ cup extra virgin olive oil
  ⅛ teaspoon salt
  Pinch of ground white pepper

  12 sea scallops (about 12 ounces), rinsed
    and dried
  2 teaspoons extra virgin olive oil
  1 teaspoon Angel Dust Cajun Seasoning
    (page 137)
  4 (½-inch thick) slices fresh, peeled, and
    cored pineapple
  1 tablespoon granulated sugar
  4 ounces arugula, rinsed and trimmed

To prepare the vinaigrette, in a small saucepan, bring the pineapple and lime juices to a boil and cook over medium-high heat for 13 to 14 minutes. As the juice reduces, the thickened syrup will spatter slightly. Reduce the heat to medium and simmer for an additional 3 to 4 minutes. Let the syrup cool for 10 minutes. Transfer the syrup, onion, honey, mustard, ancho chile powder, and garlic purée to a blender and purée until smooth. With the blender running, slowly add the oil in a thin steady stream. Season with the salt and pepper.

Heat a charcoal or gas grill.

To prepare the scallops and pineapple, drizzle the oil over the scallops, then season with the Cajun seasoning, salt, and pepper. Sprinkle half the sugar over one side of the pineapple slices. Grill the scallops for 6 to 8 minutes, turning once during cooking. Grill the pineapple at the same time by placing the unsugared side down on the grill first. After 4 minutes turn the pineapple slices over and sprinkle with the remaining sugar. Cook for 2 minutes, turn over again, and finish cooking 1 to 2 minutes more, taking care not to burn the fruit. Transfer scallops and pineapple to a platter. In a large bowl toss the arugula with some of the vinaigrette, then divide it among four salad plates. Cut each pineapple slice into eighths and place one portion onto each plate along with 3 scallops. Drizzle the scallops and pineapple with some of the vinaigrette.

Tomato Stack with Herb-Crusted Goat Cheese

Serves 4

In Chicago, unfortunately, great tomatoes like the "Creoles" grown around New Orleans are hard to come by. In the summer, though, I try to get around this problem by haunting the farmers' markets. One farmer I buy from grows twenty different types of tomatoes, more than enough to inspire a dish like this.

1 tablespoon finely chopped fresh rosemary

1 tablespoon finely chopped fresh thyme

1 tablespoon finely chopped fresh basil

1 (10.5-ounce) log goat cheese (chèvre)

2 medium red heirloom or any ripe, fresh tomatoes

2 medium yellow heirloom, or any ripe, fresh tomatoes

¼ teaspoon salt

⅛ teaspoon freshly ground black pepper

16 medium to large fresh basil leaves

½ pint small red teardrop or cherry tomatoes

½ pint small yellow teardrop tomatoes

2 tablespoons extra virgin olive oil

1 to 2 tablespoons Balsamic Reduction (page 138)

Mix the rosemary, thyme, and basil together on a flat plate. Roll the log of goat cheese in the herbs, coating all of it except the ends. With a sharp knife, cut the herb-crusted cheese into 12 slices. (If the cheese is too soft to cut, wrap in plastic wrap and refrigerate until chilled; then slice.) Set aside.

To assemble the tomato stacks, cut four thick slices, each about ⅜ inch thick, from the center section of each medium-sized tomato. Season with the salt and pepper. Place 1 slice of tomato on a large dinner plate, put 1 piece of the herb-crusted cheese on top of the tomato, then 1 basil leaf. Continue stacking in that order, alternating the color of tomato slices and ending with a basil leaf. Each finished stack will have 4 slices of tomato, 3 pieces of cheese, and 4 basil leaves.

Cut the teardrop or cherry tomatoes in half and sprinkle around the tomato stacks. Drizzle with oil and then the balsamic reduction.

CREOLE CAESAR SALAD
with Creole Caesar Dressing

Everybody loves Caesar salad. For my money, I much prefer Creole mustard to Dijon, so that's what I use—preferably the Horseshoe brand from Rex in New Orleans.

Creole Croutons
2 cups of ¾-inch cubed dried French or
   Italian white bread, crusts removed
1½ tablespoons extra virgin olive oil
½ teaspoon Angel Dust Cajun Seasoning
   (page 137)

Creole Caesar Dressing
1 anchovy fillet
1 teaspoon minced garlic
1 large egg
⅔ cup vegetable oil
⅓ cup extra virgin olive oil
2 tablespoons Parmesan cheese
2 teaspoons Creole mustard
2 teaspoons freshly squeezed lemon juice
1 teaspoon freshly squeezed lime juice
1 teaspoon water
⅛ teaspoon Angel Dust Cajun Seasoning
   (page 137)
⅛ teaspoon freshly ground black pepper
⅛ teaspoon salt

1 pound romaine lettuce, washed and cut
   into bite-sized pieces
Grated Parmesan cheese

To prepare the croutons, heat the oil in a large nonstick sauté pan over medium-high heat for 1 minute. Add the bread cubes, stirring and tossing in the pan to evenly coat the bread with the oil. Sprinkle in the Cajun seasoning while stirring continuously. Toast for 5 minutes until golden brown. Reserve for garnishing the salad.

To make the dressing, place the anchovy and garlic into a food processor, cover, and pulse on and off several times. Add the egg, and with the motor running, slowly add the vegetable and olive oils. Add the cheese, mustard, lemon and lime juices, water, Cajun seasoning, pepper, and salt; process briefly until ingredients are incorporated. Refrigerate until ready to use.

In a large bowl, toss romaine with the dressing, allowing approximately 3 tablespoons of dressing per serving. Serve on chilled salad plates; top with croutons and additional Parmesan cheese. Serve immediately.

NEW ORLEANS COBB SALAD
with Paulie's Blue-Cheese Dressing

SERVES 6

*This is almost a "gumbo salad," considering its use
of chicken, andouille, shrimp, and crawfish. The
best part is my chef Paulie' Papadopoulus's blue-
cheese dressing.*

Paulie's Blue-Cheese Dressing
- 1 large egg
- 1 tablespoon freshly squeezed lemon juice
- ¾ cup vegetable oil
- 5 ounces blue cheese, preferably Maytag
- ¼ cup heavy whipping cream
- ¼ cup sour cream
- ¼ teaspoon salt
- ⅛ teaspoon freshly ground black pepper

- 6 (6-ounce) boneless, skinless, chicken breasts
- 12 large shrimp, peeled and deveined
- 1½ tablespoons extra virgin olive oil
- 1½ teaspoons plus ¾ teaspoon Angel Dust Cajun Seasoning (page 137)
- 12 ounces crawfish tail meat, rinsed and drained
- 12 ounces andouille, sliced into ¼-inch slices and quartered
- 18 ounces baby lettuce greens, washed
- 6 hard-boiled eggs, peeled and chopped
- 2 large tomatoes, diced
- 6 ounces crumbled blue cheese, preferably Maytag

To prepare the dressing, purée the egg and lemon juice in a blender for several seconds. With the motor running on low speed, add the oil in a slow, steady stream. Add 2 ounces of the blue cheese and process until smooth. Transfer the mixture to a small bowl and whisk in the cream, sour cream, salt, and pepper. Crumble the remaining 3 ounces blue cheese and fold into the dressing. Cover and refrigerate until ready to use.

Heat a charcoal or gas grill. Place the chicken and shrimp on a large tray or jelly roll pan. Drizzle the oil over them, coating both sides. Season with 1½ teaspoons of the Cajun seasoning. Over high heat, grill the chicken for 12 to 14 minutes, turning several times during cooking. At the same time, grill the shrimp for 6 to 7 minutes. Transfer to a platter. Refrigerate until needed.

Season the crawfish with the remaining ¾ teaspoon Cajun seasoning. Cook the crawfish over medium-high heat for 2 minutes in a nonstick sauté pan; transfer to a small plate. Add the andouille to the sauté pan and cook until well brown, 4 to 5 minutes. Set aside or refrigerate if using at a later time.

Before serving, dice the chicken. To assemble the salad, toss the salad greens with some of the blue-cheese dressing and divide among large dinner plates. Scatter the egg on top of the dressed lettuce, then the tomatoes. Layer the crawfish next, followed by the andouille, the chicken, and the shrimp. Sprinkle with crumbled blue cheese and serve with additional dressing.

Soups

Chicken and Sausage Gumbo

Serves 6

Being from the Midwest, where it's so damn cold in the winter, I like my gumbo a little bit thicker than some folks in New Orleans make it. Still, here and there in Louisiana, I have tasted gumbo even thicker than mine. This Heaven on Seven signature dish has a real punch to it. It's no chicken noodle soup, that's for sure.

2 pounds boneless, skinless chicken breasts, cut into ¾-inch cubes

4 teaspoons plus ½ teaspoon Angel Dust Cajun Seasoning (page 137)

2 tablespoons extra virgin olive oil

1 pound andouille, cut into ¼-inch slices

1 cup diced yellow onion

¾ cup thinly sliced green onion, white and green parts

½ cup diced red onion

2 cups seeded, diced green bell pepper

1½ cups diced celery

1 tablespoon seeded, minced jalapeño

1 tablespoon Roasted-Garlic Purée (page 142)

½ teaspoon dried basil

½ teaspoon dried oregano

¼ teaspoon freshly ground black pepper

¼ teaspoon ground white pepper

¼ teaspoon crushed red pepper flakes

1 small bay leaf

6⅓ cups Chicken Stock (page 139)

1 cup Dark Roux (page 134)

¼ teaspoon filé powder (see note)

White Rice (page 108)

Toss the chicken and 4 teaspoons of the Cajun seasoning together in a medium-sized bowl and set aside.

In a large (7-quart) heavy Dutch oven, preferably enameled cast iron, heat the oil over high heat. When the oil is hot but not smoking, add the andouille and brown for 6 minutes, stirring frequently. Add the seasoned chicken and cook for 4 minutes; add the onions and cook for an additional 2 minutes, stirring occasionally. Mix in the bell pepper, celery, jalapeño, and garlic purée, and sauté for 2 minutes. Add the basil, oregano, ground black and white peppers, red pepper flakes, bay leaf, and remaining ½ teaspoon of Cajun seasoning; cook for 2 minutes more. Pour in the stock and bring to a boil. Whisk in the roux a little at a time and stir continuously for 5 minutes. Reduce the heat to low and simmer uncovered for 1 hour, stirring occasionally to prevent the mixture from sticking to the bottom of the pan. Remove from the heat and stir in the filé powder. (Do not let the mixture boil once you have added the filé powder.) Remove the bay leaf.

Serve with cooked white rice.

Note
Filé powder is the ground, dried leaves of the sassafras tree and imparts an unusual but pleasing flavor. It should be stirred into a dish at the end of cooking. Boiling the filé makes it tough and stringy.

To reheat refrigerated gumbo, thin with stock or water and reheat gently.

CHICKEN AND WILD MUSHROOM GUMBO

SERVES 8

Here's a more delicate gumbo, without the smoked sausage. In its place I add wild mushrooms, which give it a rich, earthy flavor. I think "rustic" and "homey" are two good descriptions of this soup.

2 pounds boneless, skinless chicken breasts, cut into ¾-inch cubes

4 teaspoons plus ½ teaspoon Angel Dust Cajun Seasoning (page 137)

2 tablespoons extra virgin olive oil

1 cup diced yellow onion

¾ cup thinly sliced green onion, white and green parts

½ cup diced red onion

2 cups seeded, diced green bell pepper

1½ cups diced celery

1 tablespoon seeded, minced jalapeño

1 tablespoon Roasted-Garlic Purée, (page 142)

1 pound assorted wild mushrooms, cleaned and stemmed

1 teaspoon Worcestershire sauce

1 teaspoon hot pepper sauce

½ teaspoon dried basil

½ teaspoon dried oregano

¼ teaspoon freshly ground black pepper

¼ teaspoon ground white pepper

¼ teaspoon crushed red pepper flakes

1 small bay leaf

7 cups Chicken Stock (page 139)

1 cup Dark Roux (page 134)

¼ teaspoon kosher salt

¼ teaspoon filé powder (see note on page 34)

White Rice (page 108)

Toss the chicken and 4 teaspoons of the Cajun seasoning together in a medium bowl and set aside.

In a large (7-quart) heavy Dutch oven, preferably enameled cast iron, heat the oil over high heat. When the oil is hot but not smoking, add the chicken and cook for 4 minutes; then add the onions and cook for an additional 2 minutes, stirring occasionally. Mix in the bell pepper, celery, jalapeño, and garlic purée, and sauté for 2 minutes. Add the mushrooms, Worcestershire sauce, hot pepper sauce, basil, oregano, ground black and white peppers, red pepper flakes, bay leaf, and remaining ½ teaspoon Cajun seasoning; cook for 5 minutes more. Pour in the stock and bring to a boil. Whisk in the roux a little at a time; cook for 5 minutes, stirring continuously. Reduce the heat to low and simmer uncovered for 1 hour, stirring occasionally to prevent the mixture from sticking to the bottom of the pan. Remove from the heat and stir in the filé powder. (Do not let the mixture boil once you have added the filé powder.) Remove the bay leaf.

Serve with cooked white rice.

Note
To reheat refrigerated gumbo, thin with stock or water and reheat gently; again, do not boil or the filé will become stringy.

STEAK GUMBO

SERVES 8 TO 10

Hey, everybody loves beef stew, but here's a version Dinty Moore never dreamed of. We take the main components of beef stew and turn them into a soup so thick it's got to be a gumbo. Down in Cajun Country, they love to put a scoop of potato salad in their gumbo; check out what happens when you put a scoop of my mashed potatoes in this gumbo. It's meat and potatoes, Jimmy style!

4½ pounds 7-blade beef pot roast, trimmed and cut into 6 sections (see note)

1 teaspoon plus 5 teaspoons Angel Dust Cajun Seasoning (page 137)

3 tablespoons extra virgin olive oil

2 cups seeded, chopped green bell pepper

1 cup diced celery

1 cup chopped yellow onion

½ cup diced red onion

½ cup sliced green onion, white and green parts

1 tablespoon seeded, minced jalapeño

1 tablespoon Roasted-Garlic Purée (page 142)

½ teaspoon dried basil

½ teaspoon dried oregano

¼ teaspoon freshly ground black pepper

¼ teaspoon ground white pepper

¼ teaspoon crushed red pepper flakes

1 bay leaf

6½ cups Chicken Stock (page 139)

1 cup plus 2 tablespoons Dark Roux (page 134)

2 tablespoons filé powder (see note on page 34)

Roasted-Garlic Mashed Potatoes (page 107)

Season the meat with 1 teaspoon Cajun seasoning. Heat a large (7-quart) Dutch oven, preferably enameled cast iron, over high heat until very hot, at least 5 minutes. Add the oil and brown the meat on all sides, 6 to 8 minutes. Transfer the meat to a platter. Reduce the heat to medium-high and add the bell pepper, celery, onions, jalapeño, garlic purée, basil, oregano, ground black and white peppers, red pepper flakes, bay leaf, and remaining 5 teaspoons of Cajun seasoning; cook until vegetables are soft, stirring frequently, about 10 minutes.

Add the stock and bring the mixture to a boil over high heat. Whisk in the roux a little at a time. Return the meat to the pot, along with any juices that have accumulated on the platter. Lower the heat to medium, cover, and simmer for 2 hours, stirring occasionally to prevent the mixture from sticking to the bottom of the pan. Turn off the heat and transfer the meat to a cutting board. Whisk in the filé powder. Separate the lean meat from the bones, cut meat into bite-sized pieces, and return meat to the pot. Discard the bones. Remove the bay leaf.

Serve with a mound of mashed potatoes.

Note
Most Dutch ovens will not accommodate an entire roast in one piece. Ask your butcher to cut the blade roast into manageable pieces. To reheat refrigerated gumbo, thin with stock or water and reheat gently.

EVERYTHING GUMBO

My thinking on this one is simple enough. One way to make sure your gumbo is a real experience is to put "everything" in it. Based on a gumbo I tasted at the old Chez Helene in New Orleans, this one has sausage, oysters, shrimp, and something the Crescent City sells as "gumbo crabs." If you can't get them, just chop up blue crabs or settle for the more subdued flavor of picked crabmeat.

- 1 pound boneless, skinless chicken breasts, cut into ¾-inch cubes
- 2 teaspoons plus ½ teaspoon Angel Dust Cajun Seasoning (page 137)

- 2 tablespoons extra virgin olive oil
- 1 pound andouille, cut into ¼-inch slices
- 1 cup diced yellow onion
- ¾ cup thinly sliced green onion, white and green parts
- ½ cup diced red onion
- 2 cups seeded, diced green bell pepper
- 1½ cups diced celery
- 1 tablespoon seeded, minced jalapeño
- 1 tablespoon Roasted-Garlic Purée, (page 142)
- ½ teaspoon dried basil
- ½ teaspoon dried oregano
- ¼ teaspoon freshly ground black pepper
- ¼ teaspoon ground white pepper
- ¼ teaspoon crushed red pepper flakes
- 1 small bay leaf
- 6⅓ cups Chicken Stock (page 139)
- 1 cup Dark Roux (page 134)
- 1 pound rock shrimp or small shrimp, peeled and deveined
- 1 pound small crab claws, such as blue crab (optional)
- 12 shucked oysters (optional)
- 8 ounces crawfish tail meat, rinsed and drained
- ¼ teaspoon filé powder (see note on page 34)
- White Rice (page 108)

Toss the chicken and 2 teaspoons Cajun seasoning together in a medium-sized bowl and set aside.

In a large (7-quart) heavy Dutch oven, preferably enameled cast iron, heat the oil over high heat. When the oil is hot but not smoking, add the andouille and brown for 6 minutes, stirring frequently. Add the chicken and cook for 4 minutes; add the onions and cook for an additional 2 minutes, stirring occasionally. Mix in the bell pepper, celery, jalapeño, and garlic purée; sauté for 2 minutes. Add the basil, oregano, ground black and white peppers, red pepper flakes, bay leaf, and remaining ½ teaspoon Cajun seasoning; cook for 2 minutes more. Pour in the stock and bring to a boil. Whisk in the roux a little at a time; cook for 5 minutes, stirring continuously. Reduce the heat to low and simmer uncovered for 1 hour, stirring occasionally to prevent the mixture from sticking to the bottom of the pan. Add the shrimp, crab claws, and oysters; cook for 2 minutes. Remove from heat. Stir in the crawfish tail meat and the filé powder. Remove the bay leaf.

Serve with cooked white rice.

Note
To reheat refrigerated gumbo, thin with stock or water and reheat gently.

TEXAS ROADHOUSE CHILI

SERVES 8 TO 10

Yee-haa! It's Texas, podnuh, so that means no beans in this chili. But there is plenty of meat, from pork loin ends to beef stew meat to ground beef. I think you'll like the taste that comes from the different types of chile peppers.

6 tablespoons vegetable oil

2 pounds beef stew meat, cut into 1-inch cubes

1¼ pounds pork stew meat, cut into ¾-inch cubes

2 pounds lean ground beef

2 cups diced yellow onion

¼ cup seeded, diced jalapeño

2 tablespoons Roasted-Garlic Purée (page 142)

3 cups water

12 ounces beer (such as Lone Star)

1 tablespoon minced chipotle chiles in adobo sauce, plus 1 tablespoon of the adobo sauce

1 tablespoon Hungarian paprika

1 tablespoon Spanish paprika

1 tablespoon chile powder

1 tablespoon ground cumin

1 tablespoon ground Mexican oregano

2½ teaspoons kosher salt

¼ teaspoon ground ancho chile powder

¼ teaspoon ground guajillo chile powder

⅛ teaspoon freshly ground black pepper

⅛ teaspoon ground white pepper

⅛ teaspoon crushed red pepper flakes

Pico de Gallo Salsa (page 106)

Heat a large (7-quart) Dutch oven, preferably enameled cast iron, over high heat until very hot, at least 5 minutes. Add 3 tablespoons of the oil. When the oil is hot but not smoking, add the beef stew meat and brown on all sides for 3 to 4 minutes, stirring frequently. Using a slotted spoon, transfer the meat to a large bowl and drain fat from the pan. Add 2 tablespoons of oil to the pan and brown the pork for 3 to 4 minutes. With a slotted spoon, transfer the pork to the bowl holding the beef; drain fat from the pan. Add the remaining 1 tablespoon of oil and brown the ground beef; this takes approximately 5 minutes. Transfer to the bowl holding the other meat. Add the onion, jalapeño, and garlic purée to the pan; sauté for 5 minutes. Add all of the remaining ingredients. Bring to a boil over high heat and simmer, uncovered, for 10 minutes. Cover, reduce heat to low, and simmer for 1¼ to 1½ hours.

Serve bowls of chili topped with a small portion of the salsa.

Note

Texas style chili usually contains lots of meat but no beans. If you like them, add drained and rinsed canned kidney, black, or pinto beans near the end of cooking. To reheat refrigerated chili, thin with a little stock or water.

TURTLE SOUP

*There are still people out there who don't know
how good turtle meat is—but most of them don't
live in New Orleans. Turtle soup is a greatest hit
there, inspiring me to come up with this blend of
Louisiana turtle, smoked tasso, and pickled pork
cooked in a veal stock and slapped with dry sherry
right at the end. You'll see why turtle soup is so
popular at all the Mardi Gras balls!*

2 pounds turtle meat, cut into ½-inch pieces
2 tablespoons plus ¼ teaspoon Angel Dust
   Cajun Seasoning (page 137)
3 tablespoons extra virgin olive oil
½ cup diced tasso ham
½ cup shredded pickled pork or Shredded
   Smoked Pork Shoulder Butt (page 141)
⅓ cup diced yellow onion
⅓ cup diced red onion
3 tablespoons thinly sliced green onion,
   white and green parts
2 cups seeded, diced green bell pepper
½ cups diced celery
2 teaspoons seeded, minced jalapeño
1 tablespoon Roasted-Garlic Purée,
   (page 142)
¼ teaspoon Hungarian paprika
¼ teaspoon Spanish paprika
⅛ teaspoon chile powder
⅛ teaspoon freshly ground black pepper
⅛ teaspoon ground white pepper
⅛ teaspoon crushed red pepper flakes
⅛ teaspoon kosher salt
1 small bay leaf
6 cups Veal Stock (page 140)
1 (5.5-ounce) can tomato juice
⅛ teaspoon Worcestershire sauce
⅛ teaspoon hot pepper sauce
1 tablespoon sherry
1 tablespoon Blond Roux (page 134)

Season the turtle meat with 2 tablespoons of
the Cajun seasoning.

In a large (7-quart) heavy Dutch oven, preferably enameled cast iron, heat the oil over
high heat. When the oil is hot but not smoking, add the turtle meat and brown for 10 minutes. Add the ham and pork; continue cooking
for 5 minutes. Add the onions and cook for
2 more minutes. Mix in the bell pepper, celery,
jalapeño, garlic purée, Hungarian and Spanish
paprikas, chile powder, ground black and white
peppers, red pepper flakes, salt, bay leaf, and
remaining ¼ teaspoon Cajun seasoning, evenly
coating the meat and vegetables with the
seasonings. Pour in the stock, tomato juice,
Worcestershire sauce, and hot pepper sauce;
bring the mixture to a boil. Reduce heat to
low and simmer partially covered for 2½ hours.
Whisk in the sherry, then the roux, and cook
until thickened, about 5 minutes. Remove the
bay leaf.

Note
*This soup gets its richness from the veal stock. You
may substitute a good chicken stock for the veal
stock, but the gumbo will not have the same depth
of flavor.*

MARTY'S SHRIMP AND CORN CHOWDER

SERVES 6

This soup became a must-cook favorite at the original Heaven on Seven on Wabash, one of those dishes we'd better have on the menu every Friday. The soup picks up incredible sweetness from the corn (especially from the sweet creamed corn) and probably from the shrimp too. This dish is named in memory of our longtime customer and friend, Marty Katz.

1 tablespoon plus 2 tablespoons unsalted butter, chilled and cut into pieces
1 tablespoon finely chopped yellow onion
1 tablespoon finely chopped red onion
1 tablespoon thinly sliced green onion, white and green parts
½ cup seeded, finely diced red bell pepper
¼ cup seeded, finely diced green bell pepper
¼ cup finely diced celery
1½ teaspoons seeded, minced jalapeño
2 teaspoons Roasted-Garlic Purée (page 142)
¼ teaspoon ground cayenne
⅛ teaspoon ground white pepper
⅛ teaspoon crushed red pepper flakes
2 (15.25-ounce) cans sweet creamed corn
1½ cups fresh or frozen corn kernels
2 cups heavy whipping cream
1 tablespoon honey
½ teaspoon kosher salt
¾ pound rock shrimp or small shrimp, peeled and deveined

Melt 1 tablespoon butter in a 4-quart heavy saucepan over medium heat. Add the onions and sauté for 2 minutes. Stir in the red and green bell peppers, celery, jalapeño, and garlic purée; cook for 1 minute. Mix in the cayenne, white pepper, and red pepper flakes; cook for an additional 1 to 2 minutes, stirring frequently. Add the creamed corn, corn kernels, cream, honey, and salt; simmer over low heat for 25 minutes. Put the shrimp into the saucepan and simmer for 2 minutes. Whisk in the 2 tablespoons chilled butter a few pieces at a time.

ROASTED POBLANO AND YUKON GOLD POTATO SOUP

SERVES 8

Chicago winters get way too cold for chilled vichys-soise, but this warm potato soup hits the spot. It's heated up in both temperature and taste. The po-blanos provide a nice kick, and the Yukon Gold potatoes produce a soup that is buttery, creamy, and smooth.

2 pounds Yukon Gold potatoes, peeled and
   cut into ½-inch cubes

3 cups heavy whipping cream

4 cups Chicken Stock (page 139)

2 roasted poblano peppers, peeled, seeded,
   and finely diced (page 142)

2 teaspoons Roasted-Garlic Purée
   (page 142)

1 teaspoon kosher salt

⅛ teaspoon ground jalapeño powder

⅛ teaspoon ground white pepper

Pinch of freshly freshly ground black pepper

2 tablespoons unsalted butter, chilled and
   cut into several pieces

Place the potatoes in a 4-quart saucepan, cover with water, and bring to a boil; simmer for 10 minutes, until tender. Drain and transfer to a food processor; add cream and process until smooth. Return the potato mixture to the saucepan. Whisk in the stock, peppers, garlic purée, salt, jalapeño powder, and ground white and black peppers. Bring the soup to a boil over medium-high heat, stirring frequently. Reduce heat to low and simmer for 15 minutes, stirring frequently to prevent the soup from burning or lumps from forming. Whisk in the chilled butter a few pieces at a time. Serve hot.

CREAM OF SWEET POTATO SOUP

SERVES 6

I like the fact that African slaves taught New Orleans, the Deep South, and finally the world how good sweet potatoes can be. These roasted and sweetened ones travel well across the Mason-Dixon line. This soup's sugary flavor and golden color are especially welcome in the fall.

2½ tablespoons unsalted butter
1 cup diced yellow onion
½ cup diced celery
½ cup peeled, diced carrot
1½ teaspoons Roasted-Garlic Purée
   (page 142)
2 pounds sweet potatoes, peeled and cut
   into ½-inch cubes
⅛ teaspoon ground cinnamon
Pinch of freshly grated nutmeg
Pinch of ground allspice
1 small bay leaf
4 cups Chicken Stock (page 139)
1 cup heavy whipping cream
1 tablespoon dark brown sugar
1 teaspoon light molasses
½ teaspoon kosher salt
¼ teaspoon ground white pepper

Melt the butter in a heavy 3-quart saucepan over medium-high heat. Add the onion, celery, carrot, and garlic purée; cook for 3 minutes, until vegetables are soft. Mix in the potatoes, cinnamon, nutmeg, allspice, and bay leaf, and stir continuously for 2 to 3 minutes, until potatoes begin to soften and spices are aromatic. Add the chicken stock, bring to a boil, lower the heat to medium-low, and simmer for 30 minutes. Remove the bay leaf. Purée the soup using a hand-held immersion blender, or blend in several batches in a blender. (If using a standard blender, place a folded dish towel over the top to prevent hot liquid from splashing out.) Pulse on and off until the soup is smoothly puréed. Return the soup to the saucepan and whisk in the cream, brown sugar, molasses, salt, and pepper. Serve hot.

JAMAICAN RED BEAN SOUP

SERVES 6

In the islands, most folks call red kidney beans "red peas." In New Orleans, red beans and rice are a staple. This red bean soup is actually a nifty way to use up leftover red beans, or you can start from scratch, as we do here. Either way, don't be shy about the jerk seasoning.

2 tablespoons unsalted butter

1 cup diced yellow onion

2 teaspoons Roasted-Garlic Purée
   (page 142)

3 cups canned red kidney beans, rinsed
   and drained

4 cups Chicken Stock (page 139)

1½ teaspoons Dry Rub Jerk Seasoning
   (page 137)

¾ teaspoon kosher salt

⅛ teaspoon freshly ground black pepper

⅛ teaspoon ground habanero chile powder

⅛ teaspoon ground coriander

Pinch of ground allspice

½ cup small diced tasso ham

½ cup shredded pickled pork or Shredded
   Smoked Pork Shoulder Butt (page 141)

1½ cups heavy whipping cream

5 teaspoons cornstarch mixed with
   5 teaspoons water

Melt the butter in a 3-quart saucepan over medium-high heat. Add the onion and garlic purée and sauté for 2 minutes, stirring frequently. Add the beans and 1 cup of the stock and bring to a boil. Reduce the heat to medium-low and simmer for 8 minutes. Carefully transfer the contents of the pan to a food processor or blender and purée until smooth. (Place a folded dish towel over the top of the blender to prevent hot liquid from splashing out.) Return the purée to the saucepan. Add the remaining stock, jerk seasoning, salt, pepper, habanero chile powder, coriander, and allspice; bring to a simmer over medium-low heat, stirring occasionally, and simmer for 10 minutes. Add the ham and pork and cook for 5 minutes. Stir in the cream, mixing thoroughly, and heat through. Whisk in the cornstarch mixture and simmer for 1 minute.

CHICKEN AND CHORIZO MAQUE CHOUX

SERVES 6

As best I can tell, this dish is Spanish, Creole, and Indian, borrowing its name from a dish of the Attakapas tribe of Louisiana. Expanding on the traditional vegetable-only maque choux (which is great, don't get me wrong), this one incorporates your basic Cajun chicken and your basic Spanish sausage. The result isn't basic at all.

½ pound bulk chorizo sausage or sausages with casings removed
1 pound boneless, skinless chicken breasts, cut into ½-inch pieces
1 tablespoon Angel Dust Cajun Seasoning (page 137)
3 tablespoons extra virgin olive oil
⅓ cup diced yellow onion
⅓ cup diced red onion
2 tablespoons thinly sliced green onion, green and white parts
1 cup seeded, diced green bell pepper
1 cup seeded, diced red bell pepper
½ cups diced celery
2 teaspoons seeded, minced jalapeño
1 tablespoon Roasted-Garlic Purée (page 142)
½ teaspoon ground Mexican oregano
½ teaspoon ground cumin
⅛ teaspoon Hungarian paprika
⅛ teaspoon Spanish paprika
⅛ teaspoon chile powder
⅛ teaspoon freshly ground black pepper
⅛ teaspoon ground white pepper
⅛ teaspoon crushed red pepper flakes
⅛ teaspoon Worcestershire sauce
1 small bay leaf
4 cups Chicken Stock (page 139)
4 cups corn kernels, preferably fresh
1 corn cob, kernels removed (optional)
1 tablespoon Blond Roux (page 134)
2 tablespoons unsalted butter, chilled and cut into pieces
White Rice (page 108)
Pico de Gallo Salsa (page 106)

Sauté chorizo in a dry nonstick sauté pan over medium heat, breaking the meat into small pieces. Drain and set aside.

Season the chicken with the Cajun seasoning. In a 5-quart Dutch oven, preferably enameled cast iron, heat the oil over high heat. When the oil is hot but not smoking, add the chicken and brown for 5 minutes. Add the onions and cook for 2 minutes. Mix in the green and red bell peppers, celery, jalapeño, garlic purée, Mexican oregano, cumin, Hungarian and Spanish paprikas, chile powder, ground black and white peppers, red pepper flakes, Worcestershire sauce, and bay leaf, evenly coating the meat and vegetables with the seasonings; cook until vegetables are soft, about 10 minutes. Add the chorizo and pour in the stock. Bring to a boil, reduce the heat to medium, and simmer uncovered for 30 minutes. Skim off any excess fat from the chorizo that rises to the surface. Add the corn kernels and corn cob and continue cooking for 35 minutes. Remove and discard the cob, whisk in the roux, and cook for 2 minutes. Whisk in the butter.

Serve in a bowl with rice and top with a portion of the salsa.

Mardi Gras Étouffée

Etouffée means "smothered" in Creole French. Smothering, or stewing, is a way both Creoles and Cajuns give intense flavor to just about anything, including crawfish, shrimp, and chicken.

2 tablespoons extra virgin olive oil
6 ounces andouille, thinly sliced
1 pound boneless, skinless chicken breasts, cut into ½-inch pieces
1 tablespoon plus ¼ teaspoon Angel Dust Cajun Seasoning (page 137)
2 tablespoons finely diced tasso ham
2 tablespoons shredded pickled pork or Shredded Smoked Pork Shoulder Butt (page 141)
3 tablespoons diced yellow onion
3 tablespoons diced red onion
2 tablespoons thinly sliced green onion, green and white parts
2 teaspoons Roasted-Garlic Purée (page 142)
1 cup seeded, diced green bell pepper
⅓ cup diced celery
2 teaspoons seeded, minced jalapeño
¼ teaspoon Hungarian paprika
¼ teaspoon Spanish paprika
⅛ teaspoon chile powder
⅛ teaspoon freshly ground black pepper
⅛ teaspoon ground white pepper
⅛ teaspoon crushed red pepper flakes
⅛ teaspoon Worcestershire sauce
⅛ teaspoon hot pepper sauce
1 small bay leaf
1½ cups Chicken Stock (page 139)
1 (5.5-ounce) can tomato juice
¼ cup Blond Roux (page 134)

8 ounces rock shrimp, or peeled and deveined small shrimp
8 ounces crawfish tail meat, rinsed, drained, and coarsely chopped
2 tablespoons unsalted butter, chilled and cut into pieces
White Rice (page 108)

In a 5-quart heavy Dutch oven, preferably enameled cast iron, heat the oil over high heat. When the oil is hot but not smoking, add the andouille and brown for 5 minutes, stirring frequently. Season the chicken with 1 tablespoon of the Cajun seasoning, add to the Dutch oven, and sauté for 5 minutes. Add the ham and pork; cook for 2 more minutes. Stir in the onions and garlic purée; cook for an additional 2 minutes. Add the bell pepper, celery, jalapeño, Hungarian and Spanish paprikas, chile powder, ground black and white peppers, red pepper flakes, Worcestershire sauce, hot pepper sauce, bay leaf, and remaining ¼ teaspoon Cajun seasoning. Stir to coat the meat and vegetables with the seasonings. Pour in the stock and tomato juice and bring to a boil. Reduce the heat to medium-low and simmer uncovered for 50 minutes. Whisk in the roux. Add the shrimp and cook for 2 minutes; add the crawfish and continue cooking for 3 minutes. Stir in the butter.

To serve, mound ½ cup of cooked white rice in the center of a plate or large bowl and spoon the étouffée around it.

Note
This makes a thick étouffée; to make it slightly thinner, decrease the roux by 1 tablespoon.

HABANERO CHICKEN JERKTOUFFÉE

SERVES 4

*Jerktouffée is the only way to describe this dish.
It has two terrific touches: the cream and butter
smooth out the Jamaican jerk seasoning, and the
usual rice served beneath étouffée gives way to corn
bread. I can't keep my fork out of this one.*

1½ pounds boneless, skinless chicken
breasts, cut into ½-inch pieces
1½ teaspoons plus 1 teaspoon Dry Rub Jerk
Seasoning (page 137)
1½ teaspoons Angel Dust Cajun Seasoning
(page 137)
3 tablespoons extra virgin olive oil
⅓ cup diced tasso ham
⅓ cup shredded pickled pork or Shredded
Smoked Pork Shoulder Butt (page 141)
1½ cups seeded, diced green bell pepper
½ cup diced celery
⅓ cup diced yellow onion
⅓ cup diced red onion
⅓ cup thinly sliced green onion, white and
green parts
1 tablespoon Roasted-Garlic Purée
(page 142)
1½ teaspoons seeded, minced jalapeño
1 teaspoon Worcestershire sauce
½ teaspoon seeded, minced habanero
pepper
½ teaspoon Hungarian paprika
½ teaspoon Spanish paprika
½ teaspoon chile powder
¼ teaspoon freshly ground black pepper
¼ teaspoon ground white pepper
¼ teaspoon crushed red pepper flakes
⅛ teaspoon ground allspice
⅛ teaspoon ground coriander

⅛ teaspoon hot pepper sauce
1 small bay leaf
2 cups heavy whipping cream
1½ cups Chicken Stock (page 139)
2 tablespoons Jimmy's Jamaican Jerk
Marinade (page 138)
½ teaspoon Dark Roux (page 134)
1 tablespoon unsalted butter, chilled and
cut into pieces
Corn Bread (page 106)

Place the chicken in a bowl and toss with
1½ teaspoons jerk seasoning and the Cajun
seasoning. Heat olive oil in a Dutch oven over
high heat. Add chicken and sauté for 3 minutes. Add ham and pork and cook for 2 minutes. Add the bell pepper, celery, onions, garlic
purée, jalapeño, Worcestershire sauce, habanero pepper, Hungarian and Spanish paprikas
chile powder, ground black and white peppers,
red pepper flakes, allspice, coriander, hot
pepper sauce, bay leaf, and the remaining 1 teaspoon of jerk seasoning; cook for 10 minutes,
until vegetables are soft. Add the cream, stock,
and jerk marinade. Bring the mixture to a boil,
reduce the heat to medium-low, and simmer
uncovered for 45 minutes. Blend in the roux,
continue simmering for 2 minutes, then stir in
the butter until melted.

To serve, place a piece of corn bread on a plate
and spoon jerktouffée over the top.

CHICKEN AND CRAWFISH ORZOFFÉE

SERVES 6

Another strange word? You bet! I grew up eating orzo in my Italian neighborhood, but my relatives also served me the Greek variation called rosa-marina—something I still order in Chicago's Greek Town whenever I get to eat there. You just mix cooked orzo with the finished product and get a super one-bowl supper.

5 ounces dried orzo, cooked according to package directions

2 tablespoons extra virgin olive oil

1 pound boneless, skinless chicken breasts, cut into ½-inch pieces

1 tablespoon plus ¼ teaspoon Angel Dust Cajun Seasoning (page 137)

2 tablespoons finely diced tasso ham

2 tablespoons shredded pickled pork or Shredded Smoked Pork Shoulder Butt (page 141)

3 tablespoons diced yellow onion

3 tablespoons diced red onion

2 tablespoons thinly sliced green onion, white and green parts

2 teaspoons Roasted-Garlic Purée (page 142)

1 cup seeded, diced green bell pepper

⅓ cup diced celery

2 teaspoons seeded, minced jalapeño

¼ teaspoon Hungarian paprika

¼ teaspoon Spanish paprika

⅛ teaspoon chile powder

⅛ teaspoon freshly ground black pepper

⅛ teaspoon ground white pepper

⅛ teaspoon crushed red pepper flakes

⅛ teaspoon Worcestershire sauce

⅛ teaspoon hot pepper sauce

1 small bay leaf

1½ cups Chicken Stock (page 139)

1 (5.5-ounce) can tomato juice

1½ teaspoons Blond Roux (page 134)

1 pound crawfish tail meat, rinsed, drained, and coarsely chopped

2 tablespoons unsalted butter, chilled and cut into pieces

Season the chicken with 1 tablespoon of the Cajun seasoning. In a 5-quart heavy Dutch oven, preferably enameled cast iron, heat the oil over high heat. When the oil is hot but not smoking, add the chicken and brown for 5 minutes, stirring frequently. Add the ham and pork, and cook for 2 more minutes. Stir in the onions and garlic purée; cook for an additional 2 minutes. Add the bell pepper, celery, jalapeño, Hungarian and Spanish paprikas, chile powder, ground black and white peppers, red pepper flakes, Worcestershire sauce, hot pepper sauce, bay leaf, and remaining ¼ teaspoon Cajun seasoning. Stir to coat the meat and vegetables with the seasonings. Pour in the stock and tomato juice and bring to a boil. Reduce the heat to medium-low and simmer uncovered for 50 minutes. Whisk in the roux; add the crawfish and cook for 5 minutes. Add butter, then stir in the previously cooked orzo.

PASTA *and* RICE DISHES

RED BEANS AND RICE

SERVES 6

This great New Orleans staple is cooked and served everywhere on Mondays—the traditional day for doing laundry. I use light red kidney beans. I also like to dice the tasso and shred the pickled pork. Though I don't mash some beans with a fork the way some Creole cooks do, I think you'll still find my red beans ultimately creamy.

1 pound dried light red kidney beans
2 tablespoons extra virgin olive oil
½ pound andouille, thinly sliced
1 8-ounce fresh pork hock
¾ cup diced tasso ham
½ cup shredded pickled pork or Shredded
   Smoked Pork Shoulder Butt
   (page 141) (optional)
½ cup seeded, finely diced green bell
   pepper
⅓ cup finely diced celery
¼ cup finely diced yellow onion
¼ cup finely diced red onion
2 tablespoons thinly sliced green onion,
   white and green parts
1½ teaspoons seeded, minced jalapeño
2 teaspoons Roasted-Garlic Purée
   (page 142)
1 small bay leaf
2 teaspoons Angel Dust Cajun Seasoning
   (page 137)
¾ teaspoon kosher salt
¼ teaspoon dried oregano
¼ teaspoon dried basil
⅛ teaspoon freshly ground black pepper
⅛ teaspoon ground white pepper
⅛ teaspoon crushed red pepper flakes
8 cups water

½ teaspoon filé powder (see note on
   page 34)
White Rice (page 108)
Chopped parsley for garnish

Soak beans overnight in a large quantity of water. Drain before cooking.

Heat oil in a 6-quart Dutch oven over high heat. Add andouille and sauté for 1 minute. Add the pork hock, ham, and pork; cook for 2 minutes. Reduce the heat to medium and add the bell pepper, celery, onions, jalapeño, garlic purée, and bay leaf; cook for 10 minutes, until vegetables are soft. Add beans, Cajun seasoning, salt, oregano, basil, ground black and white peppers, and red pepper flakes, stirring to coat mixture with the seasonings. Pour in the water, return the heat to high, and bring to a boil. Reduce the heat to low and simmer, partially covered, for 2 hours. Uncover and continue cooking about 1 hour, until the beans are cooked through. Stir occasionally, adding water if necessary. Remove from the heat and stir in the filé powder. Remove the pork hock, remove any meat attached to the bone; chop the meat finely, and stir it into the cooked beans. Remove the bay leaf.

Serve the beans in a bowl with a small portion of cooked rice; garnish with the parsley.

LINGUINE WITH JERK SHRIMP

SERVES 6

Here's another successful blending of Creole and Caribbean; any hard edges are smoothed out with cream. Just toss with pasta and it's time for reggae. Or is it time for jazz?

2⅓ cups heavy whipping cream

2 tablespoons Jimmy's Jamaican Jerk Marinade (page 138)

2 teaspoons Worcestershire sauce

1 teaspoon Dry Rub Jerk Seasoning (page 137)

½ teaspoon Roasted-Garlic Purée (page 142)

½ teaspoon kosher salt

¼ teaspoon Hungarian paprika

¼ teaspoon Spanish paprika

¼ teaspoon chile powder

⅛ teaspoon ground allspice

⅛ teaspoon ground coriander

⅛ teaspoon Angel Dust Cajun Seasoning (page 137)

⅛ teaspoon freshly ground black pepper

⅛ teaspoon ground white pepper

⅛ teaspoon crushed red pepper flakes

2 tablespoons unsalted butter, chilled and cut into pieces

1½ pounds rock shrimp or small shrimp, peeled and deveined

¼ cup thinly sliced green onion, white and green parts, for garnish

1 pound linguine, cooked according to package directions

To make the sauce, combine the cream, jerk marinade, Worcestershire sauce, jerk seasoning, garlic purée, salt, Hungarian and Spanish paprikas, chile powder, allspice, coriander, Cajun seasoning, ground black and white peppers, and red pepper flakes in a medium-sized saucepan. Over high heat, bring the mixture to a boil; then reduce the heat to medium and simmer for 15 minutes, stirring occasionally. Reduce heat to low and stir in the butter; then add the shrimp and cook for 2 to 3 minutes. Remove from heat.

Place the cooked linguine in a large bowl and toss with the jerk shrimp sauce. Garnish with the green onions and serve immediately.

Chicken Voodoo Rigatoni

Serves 8 to 10

In New Orleans, voodoo is both a serious spiritual tradition and a fanciful nickname for anything touched with magic. Hey, in most ways, the people down there are no more superstitious than the Irish, the Sicilians, or the Greeks. They just eat better a lot of the time. This dish is about going to the grocery store and buying up every kind of pepper you can find, which these days is a lot. You'll love the sweet-spicy melange that results.

2 pounds boneless, skinless chicken breasts, cut into ½-inch cubes

2 tablespoons plus ¼ teaspoon Angel Dust Cajun Seasoning (page 137)

¼ cup extra virgin olive oil

½ cup diced yellow onion

½ cup diced red onion

⅓ cup thinly sliced green onion, white and green parts

2 tablespoons Roasted-Garlic Purée (page 142)

⅓ cup diced celery

½ cup seeded, diced green bell pepper

½ cup seeded, diced red bell pepper

½ cup seeded, diced yellow bell pepper

⅓ cup seeded, diced poblano chile

¼ cup seeded, diced cubanella pepper

¼ cup seeded, diced banana pepper

1 tablespoon seeded, minced Fresno chile

1½ teaspoons seeded, minced habanero chile

1 teaspoon seeded, minced jalapeño

½ teaspoon seeded, minced serrano chile

½ teaspoon seeded, minced fingerhot chile

1 tablespoon honey

1 tablespoon granulated sugar

1 tablespoon light brown sugar

1 tablespoon dark brown sugar

¼ teaspoon Hungarian paprika

¼ teaspoon Spanish paprika

¼ teaspoon chile powder

¼ teaspoon ground allspice

¼ teaspoon ground coriander

¼ teaspoon ground turmeric

¼ teaspoon kosher salt

⅛ teaspoon freshly ground black pepper

⅛ teaspoon ground white pepper

⅛ teaspoon crushed red pepper flakes

½ cup peeled and diced ripe banana

1 (8-ounce) can tomato sauce

1 cup water

¾ cup unsweetened coconut milk

¾ cup pineapple juice

½ cup mango juice

½ cup papaya juice

⅓ cup freshly squeezed orange juice

1 tablespoon Key lime or regular lime juice

1 tablespoon Hot as a Mutha hot pepper sauce or habanero sauce (see note)

3 tablespoons unsalted butter, chilled and cut into pieces

2 pounds dried rigatoni pasta, cooked according to package directions

Season the chicken with 2 tablespoons Cajun seasoning. In a 5-quart Dutch oven, preferably enameled cast iron, heat the oil over high heat. When the oil is hot but not smoking, add the chicken and brown for 5 minutes, stirring frequently. Stir in the yellow, red, and green onions and the garlic purée; cook for an additional 2 minutes. Add the celery, peppers, and chiles; cook until vegetables are soft, about

10 minutes. Add the honey, sugars, Hungarian and Spanish paprikas, chile powder, allspice, coriander, turmeric, salt, ground black and white peppers, red pepper flakes, and remaining ¼ teaspoon Cajun seasoning; stir for 2 to 3 minutes to coat the meat and vegetables with the seasonings. Mix in the banana, tomato sauce, water, coconut milk, juices, and hot pepper sauce, until thoroughly combined. Bring to a boil, reduce the heat to medium-low, and simmer uncovered for 1 hour.

When ready to serve, stir in the butter until blended; toss with rigatoni in a large bowl.

Note

Don't let the long list of ingredients in this recipe frighten you away. This is an easy dish to prepare for company. Make the sauce ahead of time and reheat it while you boil the pasta. Get to know the vast assortment of peppers available in your market; the combination of peppers and the tropical flavors make this dish exciting. Hot as a Mutha hot pepper sauce can be ordered from Heaven on Seven's website: heavenonseven.com

CHICKEN CREOLE PENNE

Serves 8

Penne for your thoughts? Well, I know where your thoughts will be once you've tried this pasta built around spicy, red-saucy chicken Creole. It's kind of like cacciatore without the bones—each forkful can have a piece of pasta and a bite of chicken together with the fabulous sauce.

1½ pounds boneless, skinless chicken
    breasts, cut into ½-inch cubes
1 tablespoon plus 1 tablespoon Angel Dust
    Cajun Seasoning (page 137)
3 tablespoons extra virgin olive oil
2 cups seeded, diced green bell pepper
1 cup diced celery
½ cup diced yellow onion
½ cup diced red onion
½ cup thinly sliced green onion, white and
    green parts
1 tablespoon seeded, minced jalapeño
2 tablespoons Roasted-Garlic Purée
    (page 142)
1 bay leaf
1 teaspoon dried oregano
1 teaspoon dried basil
¼ teaspoon freshly ground black pepper
¼ teaspoon ground white pepper
¼ teaspoon crushed red pepper flakes
1 tablespoon cane syrup or light molasses
1 tablespoon granulated sugar
1 tablespoon light brown sugar
1 tablespoon dark brown sugar
3½ cups (2 15-ounce cans) tomato sauce
1¾ cups (1 15-ounce can) crushed tomatoes
1½ cups water
1 tablespoon finely chopped fresh
    flat-leaf parsley
1 tablespoon finely chopped fresh basil
Grated Parmesan cheese for garnish

1½ pounds dried penne pasta, cooked
    according to package directions

Place the chicken in a bowl and toss with 1 tablespoon of the Cajun seasoning. Heat oil in a 4-quart Dutch oven over high heat. Add chicken and sauté for 3 minutes. Add the bell pepper, celery, onions, jalapeño, garlic purée, bay leaf, oregano, dried basil, ground black and white peppers, red pepper flakes, cane syrup, granulated and brown sugars, and the remaining tablespoon of Cajun seasoning; cook for 10 minutes, or until vegetables are soft. Pour in the tomato sauce and crushed tomatoes and simmer an additional 5 minutes. Add the water, bring to a boil, reduce the heat to low, and simmer uncovered for 1 hour. Stir in the fresh parsley and basil; heat for 1 minute. Serve with grated cheese.

BAYOU STUFFED SHELLS
with Annamarie's New Orleans Red Gravy

SERVES 8

Pasta shells are hard to beat stuffed with just ricotta cheese, so you can imagine how good they are when we toss crawfish, shrimp, and crabmeat into the mix. But why stop there? Bread the shells, deep-fry them, and dish them up with Annamarie's red gravy. It's a reminder that "fusion" started in this country a long time before guys in white hats climbed on the bandwagon.

Annamarie's New Orleans Red Gravy

- 1¼ pounds pork neck bones
- 1½ teaspoons plus ¼ teaspoon Angel Dust Cajun Seasoning (page 137)
- 2 tablespoons extra virgin olive oil
- 1½ cups diced yellow onion
- 1½ tablespoons granulated sugar
- ½ teaspoon dried oregano
- ½ teaspoon dried basil
- ¼ teaspoon freshly ground black pepper
- ¼ teaspoon ground white pepper
- ¼ teaspoon crushed red pepper flakes
- 2 (15-ounce) cans crushed tomatoes
- 1 (15-ounce) can tomato sauce
- 2 cups water
- 3 tablespoons brewed chicory coffee
- 2 tablespoons minced fresh basil
- 1 tablespoon minced fresh flat-leaf parsley

Seafood Filling

- 1½ pounds ricotta cheese, drained
- 3 large egg yolks
- 12 ounces rock shrimp or peeled and deveined small shrimp, coarsely chopped
- 12 ounces crawfish, rinsed, drained, and coarsely chopped
- 8 ounces crabmeat, drained

- ½ cup grated Asiago cheese
- ½ cup grated Parmesan cheese
- 1 tablespoon minced fresh flat-leaf parsley
- 1 teaspoon kosher salt
- ½ teaspoon Angel Dust Cajun Seasoning (page 137)
- ¼ teaspoon ground white pepper
- 1 pound dried jumbo shell pasta, cooked according to package directions
- Italian Bread Crumbs (page 136)
- 4 large eggs
- 2 tablespoons water
- ½ teaspoon Angel Dust Cajun Seasoning (page 137)
- Vegetable oil for frying

To prepare the gravy, place the neck bones in a bowl and toss with 1½ teaspoons of the Cajun seasoning. Heat the oil in a 5-quart Dutch oven over high heat; brown the bones in the oil for about 5 minutes. Reduce the heat to medium, add the onions, and cook for 5 minutes. Add the sugar, oregano, dried basil, ground black and white peppers, red pepper flakes, and remaining ¼ teaspoon of Cajun seasoning, stirring to coat the bones and onions. Pour in the crushed tomatoes, tomato sauce, and water; bring to a boil, reduce the heat to low, and simmer uncovered for 1¾ hours. Add the brewed coffee, fresh basil and parsley; simmer for 5 minutes. Remove the neck bones. (If prepared in advance and refrigerated, thin with a little water and reheat before serving.)

To prepare the filling, mix the ricotta cheese and egg yolks together in a large bowl. Stir in the rock shrimp, crawfish, and crabmeat. Add the cheeses, parsley, salt, Cajun seasoning, and white pepper, blending until well combined.

Stuff the pasta shells. Select 24 unbroken cooked shells and fill with the ricotta and seafood filling, securing the shell ends over the filling. In one pie plate, beat the eggs, water, and Cajun seasoning; place the seasoned bread crumb mixture in another pie plate. Coat each shell with the egg mixture, then the bread crumbs; transfer to a cookie sheet.

Heat 2½ inches of vegetable oil to 350° in a heavy 4-quart saucepan. Fry shells in small batches until golden brown, 1½ to 2 minutes per batch. Drain on paper towels. Keep warm in a 200° oven until all shells are fried.

Serve 3 shells per person with warm gravy.

ORZOLAYA

SERVES 6

In the mixed-up Mardi Gras spirit of orzofée, I'd like to introduce you to orzolaya—my version of rice-based jambalaya but made with orzo pasta. I really like my jambalaya Cajun brown, without the tomatoes the Creoles of New Orleans throw in. But my wife, being Italian, loves it with tomatoes. Orzolaya is my gift to Annamarie. And it tastes terrific either hot or cold.

12 ounces boneless, skinless chicken
    breasts, cut into ½-inch cubes
¼ teaspoon plus 1 teaspoon Angel Dust
    Cajun Seasoning (page 137)
1 tablespoon unsalted butter
1½ teaspoons extra virgin olive oil
6 ounces andouille, cut into ¼-inch slices
2 tablespoons finely diced tasso ham
2 tablespoons finely shredded pickled pork
    or Shredded Smoked Pork Shoulder Butt
    (page 141)
¾ cup seeded, finely diced green bell
    pepper
½ cup finely diced celery
½ cup thinly sliced green onion, white and
    green parts
2 tablespoons finely diced yellow onion
2 tablespoons finely diced red onion
1½ teaspoons seeded, minced jalapeño
1 bay leaf
1½ cups seeded, diced plum tomatoes
1 teaspoon Roasted-Garlic Purée (page 142)
6 ounces rock shrimp or small shrimp,
    peeled and deveined
8 ounces dried orzo, cooked according to
    package directions
1½ cups Chicken Stock (page 139)

¼ teaspoon Worcestershire sauce
¼ teaspoon hot pepper sauce
⅛ teaspoon freshly ground black pepper
⅛ teaspoon ground white pepper
⅛ teaspoon crushed red pepper flakes
Freshly grated Parmesan cheese

Season the chicken with ¼ teaspoon Cajun seasoning. Melt the butter and oil in a large nonstick sauté pan over high heat. Add the andouille and sauté for 2 minutes. Add the seasoned chicken and cook for an additional 4 minutes, stirring frequently so the chicken does not stick to the pan. Reduce the heat to medium-high; stir in the ham, pork, bell pepper, celery, onions, jalapeño, and bay leaf; sauté for 3 more minutes. Add the tomatoes, garlic purée, and remaining 1 teaspoon Cajun seasoning; continue cooking for 6 minutes, stirring occasionally, until the vegetables are soft. Stir in the shrimp and cook for 2 more minutes. Stir the orzo into the mixture, pour in the chicken stock, and add the Worcestershire and hot pepper sauces, ground black and white peppers, and red pepper flakes. Bring to a simmer and cook for 3 minutes. Remove the bay leaf.

Serve on plates and top with the cheese.

CRAWFISH ARANCINI

SERVES 6

Arancini means "little oranges" in Italian; in this recipe the reference is not to the fruit itself, but to the dish's resemblance to little oranges. Old Country cooks make these with bland saffron rice with peas; I use cheesy risotto with crawfish, and I deep-fry the cakes or balls formed by the mix. The outside gets very crispy, and the inside is delicious molten lava.

4 tablespoons unsalted butter
½ cup finely diced yellow onion
3 tablespoons thinly sliced green onion,
    white and green parts
1 tablespoon Roasted-Garlic Purée
    (page 142)
⅓ cup seeded, finely diced green bell pepper
⅓ cup seeded, finely diced red bell pepper
½ teaspoon Angel Dust Cajun Seasoning
    (page 137)
¼ teaspoon kosher salt
¼ teaspoon hot pepper sauce
⅛ teaspoon freshly ground black pepper
⅛ teaspoon ground white pepper
⅛ teaspoon crushed red pepper flakes
1½ cups arborio rice
½ cup hot heavy whipping cream
4 cups hot Chicken Stock (page 139)
1 pound crawfish, rinsed, drained, and
    coarsely chopped
⅓ cup grated Asiago cheese
⅓ cup freshly grated Parmesan cheese
Italian Bread crumbs (page 136)
3 large eggs
2 tablespoons water
½ teaspoon Angel Dust Cajun Seasoning
    (page 137)

Vegetable oil for frying
Annamarie's New Orleans Red Gravy
    (page 58)

Melt the butter in a 4-quart Dutch oven over medium heat. Sauté the onions and garlic purée for 2 minutes; add the bell peppers and cook for 3 more minutes. Stir in the Cajun seasoning, salt, hot pepper sauce, ground black and white peppers, and red pepper flakes. Add the rice and stir for 1 minute, coating it with the seasonings. Pour in the cream and cook for 2 to 3 minutes, or until the cream is absorbed into the rice. Add the stock ½ cup at a time, stirring after each addition until the liquid is absorbed. This takes 25 to 30 minutes. Remove from the heat and mix in the crawfish and cheeses. Set aside until mixture is cool enough to handle comfortably.

Form the mixture into 24 small balls, about ¼ cup each. In one pie plate, beat together the eggs, water, and Cajun seasoning; place the seasoned bread crumb mixture in another pie plate. Coat the arancini with the egg, then the bread crumbs, and transfer to a cookie sheet.

Heat 2½ inches of vegetable oil to 350° in a heavy 3- or 4-quart saucepan. Fry arancini in batches of 6 to 8 until golden brown, 1½ to 2 minutes per batch. Drain on paper towels. Keep warm in a 200° oven until all are fried.

Serve 4 arancini per person with warm gravy.

ELEVEN-PEPPER LASAGNA

Sweet, smoky, and hot—peppers that taste all these ways go into this lasagna, from chipotle to habanero. The uncooked pasta sheets in this recipe cook in the flavorful steam and produce a layered dish that cuts like birthday cake. Topped with a sweetish Creole tomato sauce, this is an intensely flavored dish.

Creole Lasagna Sauce

3 tablespoons extra virgin olive oil
2 cups seeded, diced green bell pepper
1 cup diced celery
1 cup diced yellow onion
½ cup diced red onion
½ cup thinly sliced green onion, white and green parts
1 tablespoon seeded, minced jalapeño
2 tablespoons Roasted-Garlic Purée (page 142)
2 tablespoons Angel Dust Cajun Seasoning (page 137)
1 bay leaf
1 teaspoon dried oregano
1 teaspoon dried basil
¼ teaspoon freshly ground black pepper
¼ teaspoon ground white pepper
¼ teaspoon crushed red pepper flakes
1 tablespoon cane syrup or light molasses
2 tablespoons granulated sugar
2 tablespoons light brown sugar
2 tablespoons dark brown sugar
2 (15-ounce) cans tomato sauce
1 (15-ounce) can crushed tomatoes
1½ cups water
2 teaspoons finely chopped fresh flat-leaf parsley
2 teaspoons finely chopped fresh basil
¼ teaspoon filé powder (see note on page 34)

Pepper Filling

1 green bell pepper
1 red bell pepper
1 yellow bell pepper
1 orange bell pepper
2 large poblano peppers
2 jalapeños
2 serrano chiles
1 banana pepper
1 cubanella pepper
1 habanero pepper
1 tablespoon chopped chipotle peppers in adobo sauce, plus 1 tablespoon of the adobo sauce

Cheese Filling

2 pounds ricotta cheese, drained
3 large egg yolks
1 tablespoon minced fresh parsley
¼ teaspoon kosher salt
⅛ teaspoon ground white pepper
¼ cup grated Asiago cheese

1 pound dried lasagna noodles, uncooked
¼ cup grated Asiago cheese
8 ounces sliced mozzarella cheese

To make the sauce, heat oil in a 4-quart Dutch oven over high heat. Add the green pepper, celery, onions, jalapeño, garlic purée, Cajun seasoning, bay leaf, oregano, basil, ground black and white peppers, red pepper flakes, cane syrup, granulated and brown sugars. Cook for 10 minutes, or until vegetables are soft. Pour in the tomato sauce and crushed tomatoes and simmer for an additional 5 minutes. Add the water, bring to a boil, decrease the heat to low, and simmer uncovered for 1 hour. Stir in the fresh parsley and basil and heat for 1 minute. Remove pan from the heat and stir in the filé powder. (The sauce can be prepared several days in advance and refrigerated. Reheat gently, adding ½ to 1 cup of water to thin; do not allow to boil or the filé will become stringy.)

To make the pepper filling, first roast the peppers. Line the broiler pan with aluminum foil and heat the broiler. Place similar-sized peppers on the broiler pan and broil until well blistered, but not completely blackened. Turn the peppers with a pair of tongs to char them evenly; this takes 8 to 12 minutes per batch. Place the peppers in a large bowl and cover with plastic wrap. Cool for 20 minutes. Peel away and discard the charred skin; remove seeds, and stems. Dice the roasted peppers and transfer to a bowl. Add the chipotle peppers and adobo sauce and mix well. Set aside.

To make the cheese filling, combine the ricotta cheese, egg yolks, parsley, salt, and pepper in a bowl. Stir in the Asiago cheese.

Preheat the oven to 350°. To assemble the lasagna, spray a 2-inch deep 13 by 9-inch baking dish with nonstick vegetable spray. Spread ½ cup of hot lasagna sauce on the bottom of the dish, then line with noodles, breaking the pieces as necessary to fit the dish. Distribute one-third of the pepper filling on top of the noodles; spread half of the cheese filling on top of the peppers. Continue layering in the following order: ½ cup sauce, one-third of the pepper filling, lasagna noodles, the remaining half of the cheese filling, ½ cup sauce, the remaining peppers, lasagna noodles, and 1⅓ cups sauce. Sprinkle with the Asiago cheese and place sliced mozzarella cheese on top. Spray a sheet of foil with nonstick vegetable spray, cover the lasagna with the sprayed side down, and poke six holes through the foil.

Bake 50 minutes at 350°. Increase heat to 375°, remove the foil, and continue baking for 10 to 12 minutes, or until cheese browns. Let the lasagna rest for 15 minutes before cutting.

Serve with additional Creole lasagna sauce.

Note
This is a spicy-hot lasagna. The "heat" of this dish can be altered by using different combinations of hot and mild peppers.

SEAFOOD

Coconut-Crusted Shrimp
with Red Curry Sauce ~ 66

Grilled Shrimp and Andouille
with Hot Ravigote Sauce ~ 67

Crawfish and Spinach in Phyllo
with Smoked Tomato Sauce ~ 68

Rock Shrimp and Chorizo Pastitsio ~ 70

Crawfish Tamales Steamed in Banana Leaves
with Roasted Vegetable Sauce ~ 72

Bayou Chile Relleno
with Sweet Corn Cream ~ 76

Creole-Spiced Tilapia
on Tomato and Corn Bread Salad
with Basil and Lemon Vinaigrette ~ 78

Seared Halibut
with Roasted Tomato and Tortilla Sauce ~ 79

Pecan-Crusted Trout
with Creole Meunière ~ 80

Pan-Seared Cod on Skordalia
with Roasted-Tomato Cream ~ 81

Seared Tuna
with Scotch Bonnet au Poivre ~ 82

Fried-Shrimp Po-Boy ~ 83

Fried-Oyster Po-Boy ~ 84

Fried Catfish with Tartar Sauce ~ 85

COCONUT-CRUSTED SHRIMP
with Red Curry Sauce

SERVES 4

This tropical curry goes great with shrimp in toasted coconut. The trick here is toasting the coconut and boiling the shrimp first.

Red Curry Sauce
    1 cup heavy whipping cream
    ¾ cup unsweetened coconut milk
    1½ teaspoons red curry paste
    2 teaspoons honey
    ½ teaspoon Roasted-Garlic Purée
        (page 142)
    ¼ teaspoon Hungarian paprika
    ¼ teaspoon Spanish paprika
    ¼ teaspoon kosher salt
    ⅛ teaspoon Angel Dust Cajun Seasoning
        (page 137)
    Pinch of freshly ground black pepper
    Pinch of ground white pepper
    Pinch of crushed red pepper flakes
    1 tablespoon unsalted butter, chilled, cut
        into several pieces

    2 tablespoons seafood boil seasoning
    2 tablespoons plus ½ teaspoon Angel Dust
        Cajun Seasoning (page 137)
    24 large shrimp, peeled, deveined,
        and tails left on
    4 cups sweetened shredded coconut
    ½ recipe Seasoned Flour (page 135)
    3 large eggs
    1 tablespoon water
    Vegetable oil for frying
    White Rice (page 108)

To prepare the sauce, place all the sauce ingredients except the butter into a medium saucepan. Whisk over high heat until the mixture comes to a boil. Lower the heat to medium and cook, stirring occasionally, for 15 minutes, or until sauce is reduced by one-third. Whisk in the butter. Set aside; reheat when ready to serve.

In a large Dutch oven, bring 4 quarts of water to a boil along with the seafood boil seasoning and 2 tablespoons Cajun seasoning. Add the shrimp, return to a boil, and simmer for 2 minutes. Drain the shrimp but do not rinse. Set aside to cool.

Heat the oven to 350°. Spread the coconut onto a jelly roll pan and toast for 30 to 35 minutes, stirring every few minutes to ensure even browning.

In one pie plate, beat together the eggs, water, and remaining ½ teaspoon Cajun seasoning. Place the flour in another pie plate. Coat each shrimp in the flour, dip in the egg mixture, then press into the toasted coconut, giving them a generous coating. Place on a baking sheet.

Heat 2½ inches of vegetable oil to 350° in a heavy 4-quart saucepan. Fry half of the shrimp until golden brown, about 3 minutes. Drain on paper towels. Keep warm in a 200° oven until the remaining shrimp are cooked.

To serve, place a mound of cooked rice in the center of a dinner plate, place 6 shrimp around the rice, and drizzle with 2 to 3 tablespoons of the sauce. Serve with additional sauce.

GRILLED SHRIMP AND ANDOUILLE
with Hot Ravigote Sauce

SERVES 6

Here's a memorable entrée or appetizer, yet another chance for shrimp and andouille to perform together. Traditionally, the Creole ravigote sauce was based on mayonnaise and used to mask the flavor of seafood that was going bad. In this case, the seafood is good and needs no covering up, so the ravigote relies on the smooth-sweet taste of reduced cream instead of mayonnaise.

Hot Ravigote Sauce
- 1 tablespoon unsalted butter
- 2 tablespoons finely diced yellow onion
- 2 teaspoons capers, rinsed and drained
- 1¼ teaspoons Roasted-Garlic Purée (page 142)
- ⅛ teaspoon Angel Dust Cajun Seasoning (page 137)
- ⅛ teaspoon freshly ground black pepper
- ⅛ teaspoon ground white pepper
- ⅛ teaspoon crushed red pepper flakes
- Pinch of salt
- 1½ cups heavy whipping cream
- 4 teaspoons Creole mustard
- 1 teaspoon prepared horseradish
- ⅛ teaspoon Worcestershire sauce
- ⅛ teaspoon hot pepper sauce
- 1 teaspoon unsalted butter, cut into pieces

- 1 pound andouille
- 24 large shrimp, peeled and deveined
- 2 teaspoons extra virgin olive oil
- 2 teaspoons Angel Dust Cajun Seasoning (page 137)
- 12 (10-inch) skewers, soaked in water if wooden
- White Rice (page 108)

To prepare the sauce, heat the butter in a medium nonstick sauté pan over high heat, add the onion, and cook 1 to 2 minutes until soft but not browned. Stir in the capers, garlic purée, Cajun seasoning, ground black and white peppers, red pepper flakes, and salt; cook for 1 minute. Whisk in the cream, mustard, horseradish, and Worcestershire and hot pepper sauces. Bring to a boil and simmer, whisking occasionally, for 5 minutes, or until sauce thickens. Add the butter, whisking until completely incorporated. Set aside until needed. Reheat the sauce before serving.

Heat a charcoal or gas grill.

Slice the andouille diagonally into 36 ½-inch slices. Place the andouille and shrimp in a medium-sized bowl, drizzle with the oil, and toss to coat. Sprinkle with the Cajun seasoning and mix thoroughly. Thread 3 pieces of andouille and 2 shrimp onto each skewer, alternating andouille and shrimp.

Grill over high heat, turning once or twice, for 6 to 7 minutes, or until shrimp turn pink and are cooked through.

Serve 2 skewers per person with white rice and a portion of sauce.

CRAWFISH AND SPINACH IN PHYLLO
with Smoked Tomato Sauce

SERVES 6

You'll like what happens when traditional Greek spanokopita heads south to the bayou. The spinach and crawfish go so well together, and both marry well with the smoked tomato sauce on the plate.

Smoked Tomato Sauce
- ½ cup wood chips soaked in water for 20 minutes (see note)
- 1 pound plum tomatoes, cored, cut in half lengthwise, and seeded
- 1 small yellow onion, peeled and cut in half
- 1 (5.5-ounce) can vegetable juice, such as V-8
- 3 tablespoons water
- ½ teaspoon light brown sugar
- ½ teaspoon dark brown sugar
- ½ teaspoon light molasses
- ¼ teaspoon Angel Dust Cajun Seasoning (page 137)
- ¼ teaspoon kosher salt
- ⅛ cup balsamic vinegar
- Pinch of cayenne
- Pinch of freshly ground black pepper
- Pinch of ground white pepper
- Pinch of red pepper flakes
- Pinch of chile powder
- Pinch of dried thyme leaves
- Pinch of ground cumin
- Pinch of ground Mexican oregano
- 3 tablespoons unsalted butter, chilled and cut into pieces

Spinach Filling
- 3 tablespoons extra virgin olive oil
- 1 pound fresh spinach, washed and stemmed
- ½ cup thinly sliced green onion, white and green parts
- 2 teaspoons Roasted-Garlic Purée (page 142)
- 1 pound crawfish tail meat, rinsed, drained, and coarsely chopped
- ½ cup drained ricotta cheese
- ¾ cup crumbled feta cheese
- ¼ teaspoon Angel Dust Cajun Seasoning (page 137)
- ¼ teaspoon kosher salt
- ¼ teaspoon ground white pepper

- 9 large sheets fresh or frozen phyllo dough
- 6 tablespoons unsalted butter, melted

To make the tomato sauce, place the wood chips in a 10-inch cast iron pan. Put the tomatoes and yellow onion in a 9-inch disposable metal pie tin and place on top of the wood chips. Cover with a tight-fitting lid (to ensure a snug seal, loosely place a piece of aluminum foil across the top of the pan before pressing the lid firmly down; press any overlapping foil up against the lid, taking care not to let it touch the flame). Turn the heat to high and smoke the vegetables for 20 minutes. Carefully remove the pan from the heat and allow to cool for several minutes.

Transfer the smoked vegetables to a blender and purée until smooth. Pour into a medium saucepan along with the juice, water, sugars, molasses, Cajun seasoning, salt, vinegar, cayenne, ground black and white peppers, red pepper flakes, chile powder, thyme, cumin, and oregano; bring to a boil over medium-high heat. Simmer for 10 minutes, whisking occasionally. Whisk in the butter a few pieces at a time. Set aside.

To prepare the filling, heat the oil in a 4-quart Dutch oven. Add the spinach and cook for 1 to 2 minutes, stirring as it begins to cook down. Add the green onions and garlic purée; cook for 2 minutes. Add the crawfish and cook for 2 more minutes. Drain spinach mixture in a colander, transfer to a large bowl, and cool for 15 minutes. Stir in the ricotta cheese. Add the feta cheese, Cajun seasoning, salt, and white pepper and stir until thoroughly combined.

On a cutting board, cut the phyllo dough in half lengthwise. Cover with a lightly dampened towel. Working with one piece at a time, brush a sheet of phyllo dough with melted butter. Place another sheet of dough on top of the buttered one. Brush a second sheet with butter. Place a third sheet on top and brush

again. Place one-sixth (about ⅔ cup) of the filling 2 to 3 inches away from the short end of the phyllo nearest you. Form a triangle by folding one corner up to the opposite side, as one folds a flag. Continue folding up until the entire pastry is used and forms a triangle. Place on a lightly greased baking sheet or one lined with parchment paper. Repeat with the remaining phyllo dough until all 6 are complete. Tuck any loose ends of the dough under the triangles. Brush lightly with melted butter. (Pastries can be refrigerated at this point.) Bring to room temperature before baking.

Preheat the oven to 350°. Bake for 28 to 30 minutes until golden brown. Serve with warm tomato sauce.

Note
The best wood for this hickory or applewood.

ROCK SHRIMP AND CHORIZO PASTITSIO

SERVES 10 TO 12

Another Greek classic gets a Jimmy makeover. This was my Yiayia's (Grandmother's) recipe, but I decided to creolize it. Traditional pastitsio uses lamb; here, I use a blend of shrimp and the well-spiced Spanish sausage called chorizo.

1 tablespoon extra virgin olive oil
½ pound bulk chorizo
½ cup chopped yellow onion
2 teaspoons Roasted-Garlic Purée
   (page 142)
1 (8-ounce) can tomato sauce
2½ tablespoons tomato paste
2 tablespoons water
¼ teaspoon cinnamon
⅛ teaspoon ground nutmeg
⅛ teaspoon ground white pepper
Pinch of salt
1½ pounds rock shrimp or peeled and deveined small shrimp
10 ounces dried bucatini or ziti pasta,
   cooked al dente, according to package
   directions (see note)
½ pound grated kefolotiri or Romano
   cheese, with ½ cup reserved for the
   cheese sauce

Cheese Sauce

4 tablespoons unsalted butter
¼ cup all-purpose flour
2 cups heavy whipping cream, scalded
Pinch of ground white pepper
Pinch of salt
3 large egg yolks
3 large egg whites
⅛ teaspoon cinnamon
½ cup kefolotiri cheese (reserved from
   above)

Double recipe of Smoked Tomato Sauce
   (page 68)

Heat the oil in a 3-quart saucepan over high heat. Sauté the chorizo for 3 minutes. Add the onion and garlic purée; cook for 5 minutes. Add the tomato sauce, tomato paste, water, cinnamon, nutmeg, pepper, and salt, and bring to a boil. Lower the heat to medium and simmer for 20 minutes. Add the shrimp and cook for 2 minutes. Set aside to cool.

Preheat the oven to 350°. Spray a 9 by 12-inch ovenproof baking dish with nonstick vegetable spray. In a large bowl, mix the cooked pasta with all but the reserved ½ cup cheese. Add the chorizo and shrimp mixture and combine thoroughly.

To prepare the cheese sauce, melt the butter in a medium-sized saucepan over medium-high heat. Whisk in the flour and cook for 2 minutes. Add the hot cream, pepper, and salt; whisk continuously for 5 minutes. Remove from the heat and add the egg yolks, one at a time. Mix in the reserved ½ cup cheese. Set aside.

Beat the egg whites to stiff peaks and fold into the pasta mixture. Transfer to the prepared dish, distributing it evenly in the pan. Pour the cheese sauce on top, pushing it down in several places into the pasta. Tap the pan on the work surface to encourage some of the cheese sauce to flow between the noodles. Sprinkle the top with the cinnamon. Bake uncovered for 45 minutes. Increase the temperature to 375° and continue baking for 10 to 15 minutes, or until top is brown. Remove from the oven and let rest for 20 minutes before serving.

Note
Bucatini is a long, hollow pasta. A shorter version, ziti, can also be used.

CRAWFISH TAMALES STEAMED IN BANANA LEAVES
with Roasted Vegetable Sauce

SERVES 6

High drama is what you get from these tamales, a mixture of crawfish and corn masa cooked in banana leaves instead of wrappers.

Roasted Vegetable Sauce

1 small red bell pepper
1 small poblano chile
1 small jalapeño
¾ pound plum tomatoes, cut in half lengthwise and seeded
1 (½-inch-thick) slice yellow onion
1 (½-inch-thick) slice red onion
1 tablespoon pepitas (pumpkin seeds)
1 teaspoon sesame seeds
1 tablespoon packed fresh cilantro leaves
⅔ cup tomato juice
⅓ cup vegetable juice, such as V-8
⅓ cup Chicken Stock (page 139)
1 teaspoon Roasted-Garlic Purée (page 142)
1 teaspoon cane syrup or light molasses
¼ teaspoon Worcestershire sauce
¼ teaspoon kosher salt
¼ teaspoon granulated sugar
⅛ teaspoon Heavenly Blend hot sauce (see note) or other hot pepper sauce
⅛ teaspoon Hungarian paprika
⅛ teaspoon Spanish paprika
⅛ teaspoon ground coriander
Pinch of Angel Dust Cajun Seasoning (page 137)
Pinch of ground nutmeg
Pinch of ground allspice
Pinch of ground turmeric
Pinch of dry mustard
Pinch of freshly ground black pepper
Pinch of ground white pepper

Pinch of red pepper flakes
2 tablespoons unsalted butter, chilled and cut into pieces

Masa

1 pound prepared masa harina
5 ounces lard or unsalted butter, at room temperature, cut into pieces
1 cup grated Chihuahua cheese with jalapeño
½ cup corn kernels, preferably fresh
¼ teaspoon baking powder
3 tablespoons warm water

Crawfish Filling

1 tablespoon extra virgin olive oil
¼ cup seeded, finely diced green bell pepper
¼ cup seeded, finely diced red bell pepper
¼ cup seeded, finely diced yellow bell pepper
2 tablespoons finely chopped yellow onion
2 tablespoons finely chopped red onion
2 tablespoons thinly sliced green onion, green and white parts
1 teaspoon Roasted-Garlic Purée (page 142)
½ teaspoon seeded, minced jalapeño
1¼ pounds crawfish tail meat, rinsed and drained
¾ cup shredded Chihuahua cheese
¾ cup shredded Chihuahua cheese with jalapeño
2 teaspoons minced fresh cilantro
1 large egg
1 teaspoon Heavenly Blend hot sauce (see note) or hot pepper sauce
½ teaspoon Angel Dust Cajun Seasoning (page 137)

72

SEAFOOD

¼ teaspoon kosher salt
¼ teaspoon Worcestershire sauce
⅛ teaspoon freshly ground black pepper
⅛ teaspoon ground white pepper
Pinch ground cumin
Pinch ground Mexican oregano
Pinch of ground coriander

3 or 4 large banana leaves, cut into 12 (8 by
   8-inch) squares; plus additional banana
   leaves for the bottom of the pot
3 to 4 cups Shrimp Stock (page 141)

To prepare the sauce, preheat the broiler on
high. Cover the broiler pan with aluminum
foil, place the red bell pepper, poblano chile,
and jalapeño onto the pan and roast under the
broiler for 4 to 5 minutes, turning the peppers
with tongs to ensure even charring of the skin
(the smaller jalapeño will take less time). Place
in a small bowl and cover with plastic wrap or
place in a plastic resealable bag and seal closed.
Let rest for 20 minutes. Roast the tomatoes
and onions on the same broiler pan for about
6 minutes, turning them midway through. Peel
and seed the peppers. Peel the skins from
the tomatoes and remove and discard any
extremely burned pieces of onion. Place peppers, tomatoes, and onions in a blender.

In a 3-quart saucepan over medium heat,
toast the pumpkin and sesame seeds for
1½ minutes. Add seeds to the blender along
with the cilantro; purée until smooth. Pour the
contents of the blender through a strainer into
the same pan used to toast the seeds, pressing
the sauce through the strainer with a spatula,
if necessary.

Add all remaining ingredients to the saucepan,
except the butter. Bring to a boil over medium-
high heat and simmer for 8 minutes. Whisk in
the butter, several pieces at a time.

To prepare the masa, put the prepared masa
harina, lard, cheese, corn, and baking powder
in the bowl of an electric mixer. Beat on low
speed for 2 minutes. Add 2 tablespoons of the
water, increase the speed to high, and mix for
3 minutes. Before adding more water, test the
masa by dropping a small quantity of it into
a glass of cold water. If it floats to the top it
is ready to use. If it does not float, add water
a little at a time to the mixer and beat for
another minute. Test again. Repeat if necessary. Set aside.

Heat the oil in a 4-quart Dutch oven over
medium-high heat. Add the bell peppers,
onions, garlic purée, and jalapeño; sauté for
2 minutes. Add the crawfish and cook for
2 more minutes. Let cool for 10 minutes.
Add the remaining ingredients, blending
thoroughly. Remove from heat and set aside.

Trim any hard edges from the banana leaves.
Hold each piece of banana leaf over an open
flame on the stovetop for 5 to 8 seconds per
side. The leaf will change to a dull, brown
color. Place the shiny side facing down on the
work surface. Spread ¼ cup of the masa mixture over the center of the leaf, leaving 2 inches
at the top and bottom of the leaf. Spread ¼ cup
of the crawfish filling onto the masa. Fold up
the sides around the masa until they overlap;
then fold the top and bottom ends up to seal.
Set aside with overlapping edges face down to

prevent the tamales from coming apart. Continue until all are made.

In a large Dutch oven or stock pot, place crumbled pieces or scraps of the trimmed banana leaves on the bottom of the pot. Add 3 cups of the stock and bring to a boil over high heat. Place the tamales, slightly overlapping, on top of the crumbled leaves. Cover with a tight-fitting lid, lower the heat to medium, and steam for 45 minutes. Check the pot occasionally to ensure that the stock has not boiled away; add additional stock or water if necessary. Remove from pot with tongs.

Serve hot with the roasted vegetable sauce.

Note
Heavenly Blend hot sauce can be ordered from Heaven on Seven's website: heavenonseven.com. *If Chihuahua cheese isn't available, substitute Monterey Jack with jalapeños.*

BAYOU CHILE RELLENO
with Sweet-Corn Cream

SERVES 6

Another example of my Cajun-Mexican concoctions, this one stuffs the peppers with crawfish and Chihuahua cheese—a close relative of Monterey Jack studded with jalapeño, if you need a quick substitute. And the puréed corn makes an excellent creamy sauce.

Sweet-Corn Cream

1 (14¾-ounce) can cream-style sweet corn
1¼ cups heavy whipping cream
1 teaspoon honey
¼ teaspoon Roasted-Garlic Purée (page 142)
Pinch of kosher salt
Pinch of ground white pepper
Pinch of cayenne pepper
1 tablespoon unsalted butter, chilled and cut into pieces

Bayou Chile Relleno Filling

1 tablespoon extra virgin olive oil
⅓ cup seeded, finely diced green bell pepper
⅓ cup seeded, finely diced red bell pepper
⅓ cup seeded, finely diced yellow bell pepper
¼ cup finely chopped yellow onion
¼ cup finely chopped red onion
¼ cup thinly sliced green onion, white and green parts
1 teaspoon seeded, minced jalapeño
2 teaspoons Roasted-Garlic Purée (page 142)
1½ pounds crawfish tail meat, rinsed, drained, and coarsely chopped
8 ounces rock shrimp or small shrimp, peeled and deveined

8 ounces crabmeat, drained
1 cup shredded Chihuahua cheese
1 cup shredded Chihuahua cheese with jalapeño
1 tablespoon minced fresh cilantro
1 large egg
1 teaspoon Heavenly Blend hot sauce (see note) or hot pepper sauce
½ teaspoon Angel Dust Cajun Seasoning (page 137)
¼ teaspoon kosher salt
¼ teaspoon Worcestershire sauce
⅛ teaspoon freshly ground black pepper
⅛ teaspoon ground white pepper
Pinch of ground cumin
Pinch of ground Mexican oregano
12 medium poblano chiles, roasted (see Roasted Peppers, page 142)
Seasoned Flour (page 135)
3 large eggs
3 tablespoons milk
1¼ cups corn flour
1 tablespoon Angel Dust Cajun Seasoning (page 137)
¾ teaspoon salt
⅛ teaspoon Hungarian paprika
⅛ teaspoon Spanish paprika
⅛ teaspoon onion salt
⅛ teaspoon garlic salt
⅛ teaspoon freshly ground black pepper
⅛ teaspoon ground white pepper
Vegetable oil for frying

To prepare the sweet-corn cream, place all the ingredients except the butter in a medium saucepan. Bring to a boil over high heat and cook for 6 minutes, whisking frequently. Transfer the sauce to a blender and cover it with the lid. (To prevent hot liquid from splashing out of the blender, cover the lid with a folded dish towel.) On low speed, pulse on and off several times. Purée the sauce until smooth. Strain the sauce back into the saucepan through a fine-mesh strainer; simmer over medium-high heat for 5 minutes. Whisk in the butter a little at a time. Set aside. Reheat before serving.

To prepare the filling, heat the oil in a 4-quart Dutch oven over medium-high heat. Add the bell peppers, onions, garlic purée, and jalapeño, and sauté for 2 minutes. Add the crawfish, rock shrimp, and the crabmeat; cook for 2 more minutes. Let cool for 10 minutes. Stir in the remaining ingredients, blending thoroughly.

Leaving the stem intact, peel the roasted peppers. Using a small knife, slit open the side of each pepper and remove the seeds. (In order to keep the stems intact, it may be necessary to remove the inside of the pepper where the seeds and stem are connected at its base.)

Fill each chile with approximately ½ cup of the Bayou chile relleno filling and close chile around the filling. (Don't worry if the chiles pull apart in a few places; they will hold together when breaded.) Place on a baking sheet and continue until all the chiles are stuffed.

In one pie plate, beat together the eggs with the milk; place the seasoned flour in another pie plate. In a medium-sized bowl, whisk together the corn flour, Cajun seasoning, salt, Hungarian and Spanish paprikas, onion salt, garlic salt, and ground black and white peppers. Coat each chile in the seasoned flour, dip into the egg mixture, then coat with the seasoned corn flour. Transfer to a cookie sheet.

Heat 3 inches of vegetable oil to 350° in a heavy 4-quart saucepan. Fry in batches of 3 to 4 chiles until golden brown, 2 to 3 minutes per batch. Drain on paper towels. Keep warm in a 200° degree oven until all rellenos are fried.

Serve 2 per person with the sweet-corn cream.

Note
Heavenly Blend hot sauce can be ordered from Heaven on Seven's website: heavenonseven.com.

CREOLE-SPICED TILAPIA
on Tomato and Corn Bread Salad with Basil and Lemon Vinaigrette

SERVES 4

I got this idea from the Italian bread salad called panzanella. *This being a New Orleans–style recipe, though, it has to use corn bread and spicy fish.*

Basil and Lemon Vinaigrette

1 tablespoon freshly squeezed lemon juice
¾ cup extra virgin olive oil
½ teaspoon honey
½ teaspoon kosher salt
⅛ teaspoon freshly ground black pepper
⅛ teaspoon Worcestershire sauce
⅛ teaspoon hot pepper sauce
⅛ teaspoon Roasted-Garlic Purée
   (page 142)
1 tablespoon minced fresh basil

Tomato and Corn Bread Salad

4 cups of diced Corn Bread, cut into 1-inch
   squares (page 106)
½ teaspoon Angel Dust Cajun Seasoning
   (page 137)
4 cups diced ripe tomatoes, any variety
   (see note)
4 (8-ounce) tilapia fillets
2 teaspoons Angel Dust Cajun Seasoning
   (page 137)
2 tablespoons extra virgin olive oil
Balsamic Reduction (page 138)

To make the vinaigrette, place the lemon juice in a blender. With the motor running, add the oil in a slow, steady stream. Add the honey, salt, pepper, Worcestershire sauce, hot pepper sauce, and garlic purée; blend until incorporated. Transfer to a small bowl and stir in the basil. Set aside.

Preheat the oven to 350°. Place the diced corn bread on a jelly roll pan, sprinkle with Cajun seasoning, and toss to distribute evenly. Bake for 20 minutes turning occasionally. Allow to cool for 15 minutes.

Season the fish with the Cajun seasoning. Heat the oil in a large nonstick sauté pan over high heat. Add the tilapia and cook for 6 to 7 minutes, turning only once during cooking. (It may be necessary to cook the fish in two batches.)

To assemble the salad, place the toasted corn bread and tomatoes in a large bowl and dress with two-thirds of the vinaigrette. Divide among large dinner plates, place tilapia on top, and drizzle with remaining dressing. Finish with a drizzling of balsamic reduction over both the salad and the fish.

Note
Use a combination of ripe tomatoes such as plum and cherry, red and yellow.

SEARED HALIBUT
with Roasted Tomato and Tortilla Sauce

SERVES 4

You need a meaty fish for this dish but not one with a strong flavor, so halibut is perfect. Tortillas do double duty, lending their flavor to the roasted tomato sauce and adding crunch to the top.

Tomato and Tortilla Sauce
1 cup heavy whipping cream
2 roasted tomatoes (see page 81)
1 (6-inch) corn tortilla, chopped
1 tablespoon finely chopped yellow onion
1 tablespoon extra virgin olive oil
½ teaspoon Roasted-Garlic Purée (page 142)
½ teaspoon finely chopped chipotle pepper in adobo sauce
¼ teaspoon Hungarian paprika
¼ teaspoon Spanish paprika
¼ teaspoon Angel Dust Cajun Seasoning (page 137)
⅛ teaspoon kosher salt
⅛ teaspoon ground cumin
⅛ teaspoon ground oregano, preferably Mexican
⅛ teaspoon freshly ground black pepper
⅛ teaspoon ground white pepper
1 tablespoon unsalted butter, chilled and cut into pieces
2 tablespoons water

4 (8-ounce) halibut fillets
1 teaspoon Angel Dust Cajun Seasoning (page 137)
1 teaspoon salt
2 tablespoons extra virgin olive oil
Deep-fried tortilla strips, for garnish
Roasted-Poblano Mashed Potatoes (page 107)

To prepare the tomato sauce, in a medium saucepan combine all the sauce ingredients except the butter and water. Simmer over medium heat for 8 minutes. Whisk occasionally as sauce begins to thicken. Transfer to a blender and purée until smooth. Strain the sauce back into the saucepan through a fine-mesh strainer. Over low heat, whisk in the butter until melted; then mix in the water and heat through.

Season both sides of the fish with Cajun seasoning and salt. Heat the oil in a large nonstick sauté pan over medium-high heat. Fry for 7 minutes, turning only once during cooking.

Serve atop the mashed potatoes. Spoon on reheated sauce and garnish with tortilla strips.

PECAN-CRUSTED TROUT
with Creole Meunière

SERVES 4

Here's my spin on the New Orleans favorite Trout with Pecans. This dish always reminds me of my father-in-law, Sam, and my brother-in-law, Nicky, both of whom are in the pecan business.

Creole Meuniere Sauce
1 tablespoon extra virgin olive oil
⅓ cup finely chopped yellow onion
¼ cup finely chopped celery
¼ cup finely chopped carrots
2 tablespoons dry white wine
1 teaspoon Roasted-Garlic Purée (page 142)
1½ cups heavy whipping cream
½ cup Shrimp Stock (page 141)
2 teaspoons freshly squeezed lemon juice
3 tablespoons Worcestershire sauce
⅛ teaspoon hot pepper sauce
⅛ teaspoon Hungarian paprika
⅛ teaspoon Spanish paprika
⅛ teaspoon chile powder
⅛ teaspoon Angel Dust Cajun Seasoning
   (page 137)
⅛ teaspoon kosher salt
⅛ teaspoon freshly ground black pepper
⅛ teaspoon ground white pepper
Pinch of red pepper flakes
⅛ teaspoon cornstarch, mixed with
   ¼ teaspoon water
2 tablespoons unsalted butter, chilled
   and cut into pieces

Pecan-Crusted Trout
2 large eggs
2 tablespoons milk
2 teaspoons Angel Dust Cajun Seasoning
   (page 137)

1½ cups finely ground pecans
⅓ cup all-purpose flour
4 (8-ounce) red-meat (Sun Burst or Rainbow) trout fillets, boned and skinned
3 tablespoons extra virgin olive oil

To prepare the meunière sauce, heat the oil in a medium saucepan over high heat. Add the onion and sauté for 2 minutes. Stir in the celery, carrots, white wine, and garlic purée; cook for 3 minutes. Stir in the cream, stock, and lemon juice, bring to a boil, and cook for 5 minutes. Add the Worcestershire and hot pepper sauce, paprikas, chile powder, Cajun seasoning, salt, peppers, and red pepper flakes; cook over high heat for 5 minutes, stirring frequently. Reduce the heat to medium and continue to simmer for 5 more minutes. Whisk in the cornstarch mixture, then the butter, a few pieces at a time. Set aside. Gently reheat the sauce if necessary before serving.

In one pie plate, beat together the eggs, milk, and 1 teaspoon of the Cajun seasoning; combine the remaining 1 teaspoon of the seasoning, the pecans, and flour in another pie plate. Coat each trout fillet in the egg, then in the pecan and flour mixture; transfer to a cookie sheet.

Heat half the oil in a large nonstick sauté pan over medium heat. Add two of the fillets and cook for 3 minutes. Turn over and cook for 4 minutes, or until cooked through. Drain on paper towels and keep warm in a 200° oven. Add the other half of the oil and cook the remaining trout fillets. Serve with the Creole meunière sauce.

PAN-SEARED COD
on Skordalia with Roasted-Tomato Cream

SERVES 4

The garlicky Greek spread known as skordalia (score-dah-yah) looks like mashed potatoes but tastes like no mashed potatoes on earth—with the possible exception of mine. Skordalia is always served with cod at Greek funerals. It's so good, though, I can live with the association if you can.

Roasted-Tomato Cream
2 plum tomatoes
2 teaspoons extra virgin olive oil
1¼ cups heavy whipping cream
½ teaspoon Roasted-Garlic Purée (page 142)
¼ teaspoon Hungarian paprika
¼ teaspoon Spanish paprika
¼ teaspoon Angel Dust Cajun Seasoning (page 137)
⅛ teaspoon kosher salt
Pinch of freshly ground black pepper
Pinch of ground white pepper

Skordalia
1¼ pounds baking potatoes, peeled and cut into 1-inch pieces
6 slices white bread, crusts removed
4 tablespoons extra virgin olive oil
2 tablespoons Garlic Oil (page 142)
2 teaspoons distilled white vinegar
1 teaspoon Roasted-Garlic Purée (page 142)
¾ teaspoon kosher salt

4 (8-ounce) cod fillets
1 teaspoon Angel Dust Cajun Seasoning (page 137)
¼ teaspoon salt
Seasoned Flour (page 135)
2 tablespoons extra virgin olive oil

To prepare the tomato cream, preheat the oven to 325°. Line a jelly roll pan with aluminum foil. Cut the tomatoes in half lengthwise, remove the core and seeds, and rub with the oil. Place tomatoes on the prepared pan and roast, cut side up, for 20 minutes. Turn over and roast for an additional 20 minutes. Transfer the tomatoes to a medium-sized saucepan. Add the cream, garlic purée, paprikas, Cajun seasoning, salt, and ground peppers. Bring to a boil over high heat; cook for 10 minutes, whisking frequently. Carefully transfer the sauce to a blender and cover it with the lid. On low speed, pulse on and off several times. Purée the sauce until smooth. Return the sauce to the saucepan and reheat when ready to serve.

To prepare the skordalia, boil potatoes in lightly salted water for 12 minutes. Drain and cool for 30 minutes. Soak the bread in water for several seconds, then squeeze out excess water. Place potatoes, bread, olive oil, garlic oil, vinegar, garlic purée, and salt in the bowl of a food processor. Process for 25 or 30 seconds, until smooth. Do not overprocess or the mixture will become very glutinous. Keep at room temperature while cooking the cod.

Season the cod on both sides with the Cajun seasoning and salt, then dredge in the seasoned flour. Heat the oil in a large nonstick sauté pan over high heat. Cook the fish for 6 to 7 minutes, turning only once during cooking.

To serve, place a portion of the room-temperature skordalia on a dinner plate, top with the cod, and spoon the sauce over and around the fish.

SEARED TUNA
with Scotch Bonnet au Poivre

SERVES 6

Tuna is so much like steak in the pleasure it brings, why not serve it in one of steak's most famous presentations. Here, though, I crust my tuna with powdered Scotch bonnet, along with lots of black pepper and a little punch of Creole seasoning.

1 tablespoon plus ⅛ teaspoon freshly freshly ground black pepper

1 tablespoon plus ¼ teaspoon Angel Dust Cajun Seasoning (page 137)

¾ teaspoon ground Scotch Bonnet or habanero powder (see note)

¼ cup extra virgin olive oil

6 (8-ounce) tuna steaks

1 tablespoon cognac or brandy

1 cup heavy whipping cream

1½ teaspoons Worcestershire sauce

¼ teaspoon Roasted-Garlic Purée (page 142)

¼ teaspoon kosher salt

1 tablespoon unsalted butter, chilled and cut into pieces

Combine 1 tablespoon of the black pepper, 1 tablespoon Cajun seasoning, and Scotch Bonnet powder in a small bowl. Rub the spice mixture into both sides of the fish. Turn on the ventilation fan above the stove top. Heat a large sauté pan over high heat until smoking. Pour the oil onto a large plate and coat both sides of three of the fish fillets with a generous amount of the oil. Cook the tuna for 1½ minutes on each side for medium rare. Transfer the seared tuna to a large platter and cover with aluminum foil. Repeat with the remaining fillets and transfer to the platter to keep warm.

Remove the pan from the heat to add the cognac or brandy. Return the pan to the heat and lower the temperature to medium-high; add the cream, Worcestershire sauce, garlic purée, and the remaining black pepper and Cajun seasoning. Stir the sauce, scraping up any brown bits in the bottom of the pan. Cook for 5 minutes. Season with the salt and stir in the butter until melted.

Serve the tuna drizzled with a small portion (about 2 tablespoons) of the sauce.

Note

The aroma and heat from the Scotch Bonnet powder intensify when it contacts the hot surface of the sauté pan. To avoid choking, sneezing, and difficulty breathing, take care not to inhale over the sauté pan!

FRIED-SHRIMP PO-BOY

SERVES 4

In a lot of my fried seafood twists, I prefer corn flour to cornmeal—because it's not as gritty. I serve my po-boys on garlic bread in Chicago, where we don't get the wonderful crusty French bread the folks in New Orleans do. Garlic and Asiago cheese help make up for any deficiencies in the bread.

Garlic-Butter Spread
6 tablespoons unsalted butter, softened
4 teaspoons grated Asiago cheese
2 teaspoons Roasted-Garlic Purée
   (page 142)
½ teaspoon chopped fresh parsley
Pinch of salt
Pinch of freshly ground black pepper

4 (6-inch) deli-style or hoagie rolls, split
   lengthwise
20 ounces rock shrimp or small shrimp,
   peeled and deveined
¼ cup hot pepper sauce
Seasoned Flour (page 135)
2 cups shredded lettuce
1 tomato, thinly sliced
Vegetable oil for frying
½ recipe Honey-Jalapeño Dressing
   (page 111)

To make the garlic-butter spread, combine all the ingredients in a small bowl. Spread the cut side of each roll with the garlic butter.

Heat a large nonstick sauté pan over medium heat. Toast the buttered side of each roll for 2 minutes; flip over and toast the outside for 1 minute. Set aside.

Heat 2½ inches of vegetable oil to 350° in a heavy 4-quart saucepan. Place the shrimp in a medium-sized bowl, pour in the hot pepper sauce, and let marinate for 5 minutes. Coat the shrimp with the flour, shaking off any excess. Stirring to keep the shrimp moving in the oil, fry until golden brown, about 2 minutes per batch. Drain on paper towels. Sprinkle with salt if desired. Keep warm in a 200° oven until all shrimp are fried.

To serve, place lettuce and tomato on the toasted rolls. Divide the shrimp equally among the rolls and serve with the dressing.

FRIED-OYSTER PO-BOY

SERVES 4

As with shrimp, corn flour works better than corn-meal here. Best of all, I love using my honey-jalapeño dressing in place of humdrum mayo or tartar sauce.

Garlic-Butter Spread (page 83)
4 6-inch deli-style or hoagie rolls, split
   lengthwise
24 medium-sized shucked oysters
2 teaspoons plus ½ teaspoon Angel Dust
   Cajun Seasoning, (page 137)
Seasoned Corn Flour (page 135)
2 large eggs
1 tablespoon water
2 cups shredded lettuce
1 tomato, thinly sliced
Vegetable oil for frying
½ recipe Honey-Jalapeno Dressing
   (page 111)

Spread the cut side of each roll with the garlic butter. Heat a large nonstick sauté pan over medium heat. Toast the buttered side of each roll for 2 minutes; flip over and toast the outside for 1 minute. Set aside.

Heat 2½ inches of vegetable oil to 350° in a heavy 4-quart saucepan. Season the oysters with 2 teaspoons of Cajun seasoning. Place the seasoned flour in one pie plate; in another, beat together the eggs, water, and remaining ½ teaspoon Cajun seasoning. Coat each oyster in the seasoned corn flour, dip into the egg mixture, and coat again with the flour. Stirring to keep the oysters moving in the oil, fry 3 minutes per batch, until golden brown. Drain on paper towels. Sprinkle with salt if desired. Keep warm in a 200° oven until all oysters are fried.

To serve, place lettuce and tomato on the toasted rolls. Divide the oysters equally among the rolls and serve with the dressing.

FRIED CATFISH WITH TARTAR SAUCE

SERVES 4

Ever since we started offering it, fried catfish has been a big seller at Heaven on Seven. In my kitchen full of Hispanic chefs and line cooks, "un gato" is one of the orders we hear called round the clock. You can use tartar sauce and be happy, or upgrade to my honey-jalapeño dressing. Or go all the way with Cajun coleslaw. The best sides for fried catfish are soul-food collard greens, red beans, and black-eyed peas, each splashed with a few drops of vinegar.

Tartar Sauce
- ⅔ cup mayonnaise
- 4 teaspoons sweet pickle relish
- 4 teaspoons finely chopped green Spanish olives
- 2 teaspoons minced green onion, green and white parts
- ½ teaspoon minced fresh parsley
- ½ teaspoon freshly squeezed lemon juice
- ⅛ teaspoon Worcestershire sauce
- ⅛ teaspoon hot pepper sauce
- ⅛ teaspoon Angel Dust Cajun Seasoning (page 137)
- Pinch of dried dill
- Pinch of cayenne pepper

- 4 (8-ounce) catfish fillets
- 2 teaspoons plus ½ teaspoon Angel Dust Cajun Seasoning (page 137)
- Seasoned Corn Flour (page 135)
- 2 large eggs
- 1 tablespoon water
- Vegetable oil for frying

To make tartar sauce, combine all ingredients in a small bowl, cover, and refrigerate for at least 1 hour, or until needed.

Heat 2½ inches of vegetable oil to 350° in a heavy 4-quart saucepan. Cut each fish fillet into 4 pieces. Season both sides of the fish with 2 teaspoons of the Cajun seasoning. Place the seasoned flour in one pie plate; in another, beat together the eggs, water, and remaining ½ teaspoon Cajun seasoning. Dredge each piece of fish with the seasoned corn flour, dip into the egg mixture, and coat again with the flour. Fry until golden brown, 5 to 6 minutes per batch. Drain on paper towels. Sprinkle with salt if desired. Keep warm in a 200° oven until all fish is fried.

Serve 4 pieces per person with tartar sauce.

Note
This recipe could also be used to make catfish po-boys. Spread sandwich rolls with the garlic butter spread on page 83.

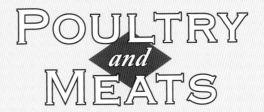

POULTRY and MEATS

PANÉED SESAME-CRUSTED CHICKEN BREAST
WITH CREOLE MUSTARD CREAM ~ 88

CHICKEN AND ANDOUILLE ROASTED CHILE RELLENO
WITH CARLOS' FAMOUS MOLE SAUCE ~ 90

GRILLED CHICKEN AND JIMMY'S OLIVE SALAD
PO-BOY ~ 92

CHICKEN-FRIED STEAK
WITH COUNTRY CREAM GRAVY ~ 93

CANE-SYRUP-ROASTED DUCK BREAST
WITH SWEET POTATO POLENTA ~ 95

JIMMY'S PANÉED BIG-ASS PORK CHOP
WITH WILD-MUSHROOM AND TASSO GRAVY ~ 96

JERK PORK AND PORTOBELLO STACK
WITH JERK CREAM ~ 98

SWEET-HOT BARBECUE RIBS ~ 100

GRILLED VEAL CHOP WITH VEAL REDUCTION
AND ROASTED-POBLANO BREAD PUDDING ~ 101

GRILLED FILET MIGNON
WITH CHIPOTLE BLACK PEPPER SAUCE ~ 102

STEAK PO-BOY WITH
GRILLED BELL PEPPERS AND ONIONS ~ 103

PANÉED SESAME-CRUSTED CHICKEN BREAST
with Creole Mustard Cream

I got the idea for this dish from chef Frank Brigt-sen in New Orleans, a master at panéeing meats (especially rabbit). The point is to make the crust crunchier and the inside moister than is possible with any kind of frying. This is a soul-warming dish, especially served with mashed potatoes and collard greens.

Creole Mustard Cream

1¼ cups heavy whipping cream
2 tablespoons Creole mustard
1 teaspoon Roasted-Garlic Purée
   (page 142)
⅛ teaspoon Worcestershire sauce
⅛ teaspoon hot pepper sauce
⅛ teaspoon kosher salt
⅛ teaspoon ground white pepper
¼ teaspoon cornstarch mixed with
   ½ teaspoon water
1 tablespoon unsalted butter

Sesame Bread Crumbs

2 cups dried bread crumbs
¼ cup sesame seeds
2¾ teaspoons Angel Dust Cajun Seasoning
   (page 137)
4 (6-ounce) boneless, skinless chicken
   breasts
1¼ cups Seasoned Flour (page 135)
2 large eggs
1 tablespoon water
1 cup canola oil

To prepare the mustard cream, in a medium saucepan, whisk together the cream, mustard, garlic purée, Worcestershire sauce, hot pepper sauce, salt, and pepper. Bring the contents of the pan to a boil over medium-high heat and simmer, whisking occasionally, for 11 minutes. Reduce the heat to low, stir in the cornstarch mixture, and heat until sauce thickens, about 30 seconds. Whisk in the butter. Set aside.

To make the sesame bread crumbs, combine the bread crumbs, sesame seeds, and 2 teaspoons of the Cajun seasoning in a pan large enough to hold the chicken breasts. Set aside.

Place a chicken breast on a cutting board. With a sharp knife, carefully butterfly the breast by slicing across the breast horizontally from the thinner end toward the thicker portion without cutting all the way through it. Open the chicken as if it were one large piece, place it between 2 pieces of plastic wrap; using a meat mallet, pound it to a thickness of ¼ inch. Continue with the remaining pieces. Transfer the chicken to a jelly roll pan and season both sides of the meat with ½ teaspoon Cajun seasoning.

Place the seasoned flour in a medium-sized pan. Beat the eggs, water, and remaining ¼ teaspoon Cajun seasoning in a pie plate.

In a 12-inch cast-iron pan or a large nonstick sauté pan, heat the oil over medium heat. While the oil is heating, bread each piece of chicken by dredging it in the seasoned flour, dipping it into the egg mixture, then coating it with the sesame bread crumbs. Return each piece to the jelly roll pan until ready to cook. Fry pieces one at a time until golden brown, about 5 minutes, turning once halfway through. Transfer to a heat-proof platter and keep warm in a 200° oven until remaining chicken is cooked.

Serve with the Creole mustard cream.

CHICKEN AND ANDOUILLE ROASTED CHILE RELLENO
with Carlos' Famous Mole Sauce

SERVES 6

Here's a dish made by the talented chef Carlos Gramajo, who was with me more than sixteen years and served as my eyes and ears at the Wabash location. This chile is roasted, then stuffed, then roasted again. And Carlos made the best mole I've ever tasted, rich in chocolate and hints of dried fruit.

Carlos' Famous Mole Sauce

Half of a 6-inch corn tortilla, torn into 6 pieces
2 pieces dried apricots or plums, or prunes
1 teaspoon golden raisins
2 teaspoons pepitas (pumpkin seeds)
1 teaspoon slivered almonds
⅛ teaspoon sesame seeds
1 teaspoon ancho chile powder
1 teaspoon guajillo chile powder
1 teaspoon New Mexico chile powder
1 teaspoon pasilla chile powder
Pinch of ground cinnamon
Pinch of ground nutmeg
1½ cups Chicken Stock (page 139)
⅓ cup diced, seeded, plum tomatoes
⅓ cup heavy whipping cream
2 wedge-shaped sections of Abuelita Mexican chocolate drink disks, chopped (see note)
2 tablespoons unsalted butter cut into several pieces, or lard

Chile Relleno Filling

1¾ pounds skinless, boneless, chicken breast, cut into ½-inch pieces
1 tablespoon Angel Dust Cajun Seasoning (page 137)

4 tablespoons olive oil
8 ounces andouille sausage, finely diced
⅓ cup seeded, finely diced green bell pepper
⅓ cup seeded, finely diced red bell pepper
⅓ cup seeded, finely diced yellow bell pepper
¼ cup finely chopped yellow onion
¼ cup finely chopped red onion
¼ cup thinly sliced green onion, white and green parts
1 teaspoon minced jalapeño
1 tablespoon Roasted-Garlic Purée (page 142)
1 tablespoon minced fresh cilantro
2 teaspoons Heavenly Blend hot sauce (see note) or hot pepper sauce
1 teaspoon Worcestershire sauce
½ teaspoon kosher salt
⅛ teaspoon freshly ground black pepper
⅛ teaspoon ground white pepper
⅛ teaspoon ground cumin
⅛ teaspoon ground Mexican oregano
1½ cups shredded Chihuahua cheese
1½ cups shredded Chihuahua cheese with jalapeño
1 large egg

12 medium poblano chiles, roasted, stems intact (see Roasted Peppers, page 142)
½ cup water

Heat a medium nonstick sauté pan over high heat. Add the tortilla pieces, apricots, raisins, pepitas, almonds, and sesame seeds. Shake the pan back and forth, toasting lightly, for 4 minutes. Add the ancho, guajillo, New Mexico, and pasilla chile powders, cinnamon, and nutmeg and toast for 45 seconds. Transfer to a blender, add the stock and tomatoes, and purée until smooth. Strain through a fine-mesh strainer into a medium saucepan. Add the cream and bring to a boil over medium heat. Add the chocolate and stir until melted. Continue cooking for 12 minutes, whisking frequently. Stir in the butter until blended. Set aside.

Place the chicken in a bowl and season with the Cajun seasoning. Heat the oil in a 4-quart Dutch oven over medium-high heat. Sauté the andouille for 2 minutes; then add the seasoned chicken and sauté for 8 minutes. Stir in the bell peppers, onions, jalapeño, and garlic purée, and sauté for 2 minutes. Add the cilantro, hot pepper sauce, Worcestershire sauce, salt, black and white peppers, cumin, and oregano; cook for 1 more minute. Let cool for 10 minutes. Mix in the cheese and egg, blending thoroughly.

Preheat the oven to 400°.

Peel the roasted peppers, leaving the stems intact. Using a small knife, slit open the side of each pepper and remove the seeds. (In order to keep the stem intact, it may be necessary to remove the inside of the pepper where the seeds and stem are connected at its base.) Fill each chile with approximately ½ cup of the chile relleno filling and close chile around the filling. (Don't worry if the chiles pull apart in a few places. They will hold together when baked.) Place in a 12 by 15-inch baking pan. Continue until all the chiles are stuffed, placing them side by side in the pan. Add the

waterto the pan, cover with aluminum foil, and bake for 15 minutes.

Serve 2 per person with the mole sauce.

Notes
Abuelita Mexican chocolate drink mix comes packaged in a 19-ounce box. Each tablet is individually wrapped and scored into wedge-shape sections. The mix contains sugar and is flavored with cinnamon. It can be found at Mexican and Latin American markets and in the ethnic-food sections of many grocery stores.

Heavenly Blend hot sauce can be ordered from Heaven on Seven's website: heavenonseven.com.

Grilled Chicken and Jimmy's Olive Salad Po-Boy

SERVES 4

There can never be enough uses for the olive salad associated in New Orleans with muffalettas. Maybe because I'm not from there (but did grow up in an Italian neighborhood!), I see olive salad as more than a one-use item.

Jimmy's Olive Salad

1 cup coarsely chopped, pitted, large green Greek olives (with herbs and marinated in oil)

1 cup coarsely chopped queen-size Manzanilla olives with pimentos

1 (15.5-ounce) jar marinated vegetables (in vinegar), drained and chopped into small pieces

1 tablespoon minced fresh parsley

1 tablespoon Roasted-Garlic Purée (page 142)

2 teaspoons capers, drained and rinsed

¼ teaspoon dried oregano

½ cup plus 1 tablespoon extra virgin olive oil

⅛ teaspoon salt

⅛ teaspoon freshly ground black pepper

⅛ teaspoon ground white pepper

⅛ teaspoon crushed red pepper flakes

Garlic-Butter Spread (page 83)

4 (6-inch) deli-style or hoagie rolls, split lengthwise

Grilled Chicken

4 (7 to 8-ounce) boneless, skinless, chicken breasts

½ teaspoon Angel Dust Cajun Seasoning (page 137)

¼ teaspoon salt

¼ teaspoon freshly ground black pepper

2 teaspoons olive oil

To prepare the olive salad, combine all ingredients thoroughly. Cover and refrigerate for at least 4 hours to allow the salad to marinate. Store in a container with a tight-fitting lid.

Spread the cut side of each roll with the garlic butter. Place on a heat-proof tray, such as a jelly roll pan, and set aside.

Season the chicken on both sides with the Cajun seasoning, salt, and pepper; then drizzle with the oil.

Heat a charcoal or gas grill. Grill the chicken over high heat for 10 to 12 minutes, turning occasionally. While the chicken is cooking, grill the buttered side of the rolls for 1 to 1½ minutes. Flip the rolls over and grill the outside for 30 seconds. Transfer the rolls to the tray. To assemble, place a chicken breast on half of each roll, top with ⅓ cup of the olive salad and the second half of the roll.

Note
This recipe makes about 4 cups of olive salad, too much for four sandwiches. Use the extra as a side dish at other meals; it keeps for a long time in the refrigerator.

CHICKEN-FRIED STEAK
with Country Cream Gravy

SERVES 4

I don't guess the South would be the South without chicken-fried steak. I go the original one better, of course. Instead of grabbing round steak and pounding it to death, I use New York strip. And instead of standard-issue milk, I use heavy cream. The result is everything chicken-fried steak is supposed to be, except with better meat and better gravy.

Country Cream Gravy

1¼ cups heavy whipping cream

¾ cup Chicken Stock (page 143)

½ teaspoon Roasted-Garlic Purée (page 142)

¼ teaspoon kosher salt

⅛ teaspoon onion powder

⅛ teaspoon freshly ground black pepper

Pinch of ground white pepper

5 teaspoons Blond Roux (page 134)

4 (8-ounce) thin, boneless, New York strip steaks, trimmed

2 teaspoons plus ½ teaspoon Angel Dust Cajun Seasoning (page 137)

Double recipe of Seasoned Flour (page 135)

4 large eggs

2 tablespoons water

1½ cups canola oil

To prepare the gravy, place the cream, stock, garlic purée, salt, onion powder, and black and white peppers in a medium saucepan and simmer for 7 minutes over medium heat. Whisk in the roux and heat until thick, about 2 minutes.

Place one steak between 2 pieces of plastic wrap; using a meat mallet, pound it to a thickness of ¼ inch. Continue with the remaining pieces. Transfer the steaks to a jelly roll pan and season both sides of the meat with the 2 teaspoons Cajun seasoning.

Place the seasoned flour in an 8 by 12-inch pan. Beat the eggs, water, and remaining ½ teaspoon Cajun seasoning in a pie plate.

In a 12-inch cast-iron pan or large nonstick sauté pan, heat the oil over medium heat. While the oil is heating, bread each piece of meat by dredging it in the seasoned flour, dipping it into the egg mixture, then coating it again with the seasoned flour. Return each piece to the jelly roll pan until ready to cook. Fry pieces one at a time until golden brown, about 4 minutes, turning once halfway through. Transfer to a heat-proof platter and keep warm in a 200° oven until all steaks are cooked.

CANE-SYRUP-ROASTED DUCK BREAST
with Sweet Potato Polenta

SERVES 4

Like most people, I associate game dishes with the fall. For this autumnal favorite, I roast the duck breast coated with cane syrup, then slice it on the diagonal and arrange it around polenta. It's got sweetness and tanginess—by now, you know how much I like that.

Sweet Potato Polenta
- 10 ounces sweet potatoes, peeled and cut into 2-inch pieces
- 3 tablespoons maple syrup
- 1⅓ cups heavy whipping cream
- 2 tablespoons unsalted butter
- ¼ cup instant polenta
- ⅛ teaspoon salt
- Pinch of white pepper

- 4 (8-ounce) boneless, skinless duck breasts
- ½ teaspoon plus ⅛ teaspoon Angel Dust Cajun Seasoning (page 137)
- ¼ teaspoon salt
- ⅛ teaspoon freshly ground black pepper
- ½ cup Chicken Stock (page 139)
- ¼ cup cane syrup
- 1 tablespoon hot pepper sauce
- Pinch of ground jalapeño powder
- 1 tablespoon unsalted butter, chilled and cut into several pieces
- 1 teaspoon port

Preheat the oven to 350°.

To prepare the polenta, place the potatoes in a small baking pan, toss with the maple syrup, and cover with aluminum foil. Bake for 30 to 45 minutes, until soft. Scrape potatoes and syrup into the bowl of a food processor and process until smooth. Heat the cream and butter over medium heat in a 3-quart saucepan. When the cream begins to simmer, slowly whisk in the polenta. Add the salt and pepper and continue stirring for 7 minutes. Mix in the puréed sweet potatoes until completely incorporated and heat through. Cover and set aside.

Heat a large sauté pan over high heat until very hot. Season the duck with the ½ teaspoon Cajun seasoning, salt, and pepper. Sear the duck in the dry pan for 1½ minutes on each side. Remove the duck to a plate. Deglaze the pan with the chicken stock. Add the cane syrup, hot pepper sauce, jalapeño powder, and remaining ⅛ teaspoon Cajun seasoning. Reduce the heat to medium and cook until syrup thickens, about 3 minutes. Whisk in the butter and port. Reduce the heat to low, return the duck to the pan along with any juices that have accumulated on the plate, and baste the duck breasts with the syrup for 2 to 3 minutes for medium rare.

Serve over warm sweet potato polenta with a drizzling of the sauce.

JIMMY'S PANÉED BIG-ASS PORK CHOP
with Wild-Mushroom and Tasso Gravy

SERVES 4

Excuse the language, but in this case the candid "kitchen talk" is more than justified. You start with a large chop, then you pound it out till it's mammoth. Breaded and panéed, it comes out tender and juicy, under a warm blanket of mushroom cream gravy. I generally use shiitakes, but chanterelle, oyster, and crimini mushrooms all work great.

Wild Mushroom and Tasso Gravy

  2 tablespoons unsalted butter
  ⅓ cup diced tasso ham
  1 tablespoon minced shallots
  1 teaspoon Roasted-Garlic Purée (page 142)
  1 large portobello mushroom, cleaned,
    stemmed, and gills scraped off (see note)
  ¼ pound crimini mushrooms, cleaned,
    stemmed, and thinly sliced
  ¼ pound shiitake mushrooms, cleaned,
    stemmed, and thinly sliced
  1½ cups heavy whipping cream
  ½ cup Chicken Stock (page 139)
  ⅛ teaspoon freshly ground black pepper
  ⅛ teaspoon ground white pepper
  ⅛ teaspoon kosher salt
  1½ teaspoons Blond Roux (page 134)

  4 (10-ounce) pork rib chops, "frenched"
    (see note)
  2½ teaspoons Angel Dust Cajun Seasoning
    (page 137)
  Seasoned Flour (page 135)
  4 large eggs, beaten
  1 tablespoon water
  Italian Bread crumbs (page 136)
  1 cup canola oil for frying
  Roasted-Garlic Mashed Potatoes (page 107)

To make the gravy, melt the butter over medium heat in a medium saucepan. Add the ham, shallots, and garlic purée and sauté for 3 minutes. Add the assorted mushrooms and cook for 5 minutes, until soft. Pour in the cream and stock, and season with the peppers and salt. Bring to a simmer and stir occasionally for 5 minutes. Whisk in the roux and cook for 2 minutes until gravy thickens. Keep warm over low heat.

Place one pork chop between 2 large pieces of plastic wrap; using a meat mallet, pound the meat to a thickness of ¼ inch, keeping the bone intact (see note). Continue with the remaining pieces. Transfer the chops to a jelly roll pan and season both sides of the meat with 2 teaspoons of the Cajun seasoning.

Place the seasoned flour in an 8 by 12-inch pan. Beat the eggs, water, and remaining ½ teaspoon Cajun seasoning in an 8 by 8-inch pan, and place the bread crumbs in another pan large enough to hold the pounded-out meat.

In a 12-inch cast-iron pan or large nonstick sauté pan, heat the oil over medium heat. While the oil is heating, bread each piece of meat by dredging it in the seasoned flour, dipping it into the egg mixture, then coating it with the seasoned bread crumbs. Return each piece to the jelly roll pan until ready to cook. Fry pieces one at a time until golden brown, about 4 minutes. Press the bone into the oil using a pair of tongs and turn the chop once after about 2 minutes. Transfer to a heat-proof platter and keep warm in a 200° oven until remaining chops are cooked.

Serve with the roasted-garlic mashed potatoes smothered in the gravy.

Note

To clean portobello mushroom caps, remove the stem, and with the tip of a spoon, scrape away the gills from the underside of the mushroom (see Jerk Pork and Portobello Stack, page 98).

"Frenching," or pounding out the meat of a chop while it is still attached to the bone, is an upper-body workout but a great way to release the day's tension. I like to say, "pound the hell out of it and you'll get one big-ass chop!"

JERK PORK AND PORTOBELLO STACK
with Jerk Cream

SERVES 6

This is it: the jerk that launched a thousand ships. And I don't mean some old admiral either. It's my take on the pepper-crusted pork sold by roadside vendors all over Jamaica, the ultimate in sweet and hot. I envision this, believe it or not, as a stack of pancakes: the pork and portobellos as the cakes, the jerk sauce dripping down the sides like syrup. Don't laugh. You'll love it!

2 pounds trimmed pork tenderloin
1 teaspoon Dry Rub Jerk Seasoning
  (page 137)
¼ cup Jimmy's Jamaican Jerk Marinade
  (page 138)

Jerk Cream
2½ cups heavy whipping cream
1 tablespoon Jimmy's Jamaican Jerk
  Marinade (page 138)
2 teaspoons Worcestershire sauce
½ teaspoon Roasted-Garlic Purée
  (page 142)
½ teaspoon kosher salt
¼ teaspoon Hungarian paprika
¼ teaspoon Spanish paprika
¼ teaspoon chile powder
⅛ teaspoon Angel Dust Cajun Seasoning
  (page 137)
⅛ teaspoon freshly ground black pepper
⅛ teaspoon ground white pepper
⅛ teaspoon crushed red pepper flakes
2 tablespoons unsalted butter, chilled and
  cut into pieces

18 (3-inch diameter) portobello mushrooms
3 tablespoons plus 2 tablespoons extra
  virgin olive oil
2½ tablespoons Angel Dust Cajun
  Seasoning (page 137)
White Rice (page 108)

Rub the pork tenderloin with the jerk seasoning and place in a large plastic resealable bag. Add the jerk marinade to coat the meat, and marinate in the refrigerator for at least 8 hours and up to 24 hours.

To make the jerk cream, combine all ingredients except the butter in a medium saucepan over high heat. When the mixture comes to a boil, reduce the heat to medium and simmer, stirring occasionally, for 15 minutes. Strain the sauce through a fine-mesh strainer, return it to the saucepan, and stir in the butter. Set aside. (If refrigerating the sauce overnight, gently reheat for 1 minute, whisk in 1 tablespoon cold water, and continue whisking over low heat until sauce is heated through. Do not boil.)

Clean the mushrooms. Remove the stem, and with the tip of a spoon, scrape away the gills from the underside of each mushroom. Drizzle with 3 tablespoons of the oil.

When ready to cook, heat a charcoal or gas grill.

Remove the pork from the plastic bag, discarding the unused marinade. Slice the tenderloin into eighteen portions. Working with one section at a time, place a piece of pork between two pieces of plastic wrap and pound out to a thickness of ⅛ inch. Complete the process with the remaining tenderloin pieces. Season the meat with the Cajun seasoning and drizzle with the remaining 2 tablespoons oil. Over high heat, grill the mushrooms for 7 to 8 minutes and the pork for 4 to 5 minutes, turning occasionally. Transfer to a platter.

To serve, place a bed of rice on each plate. On top of the rice, create the "stack" by alternating the pork tenderloin and portobello mushrooms, using three pieces of each. Ladle some of the sauce on top of the stack and around the rice.

SWEET-HOT BARBECUE RIBS

SERVES 4 TO 6

Don't try to convince me that any ingredient used in the barbecue sauce on these wonderful ribs doesn't carry its own weight. You'll be amazed at what happens when all these sweet and peppery flavors work together.

Sweet-Hot Barbecue Sauce
  3 cups ketchup
  ¾ cup water
  ¼ cup dark brown sugar
  ¼ cup light brown sugar
  1 tablespoon honey
  1½ teaspoons granulated sugar
  1 teaspoon Worcestershire sauce
  ½ teaspoon white vinegar
  ½ teaspoon freshly squeezed lemon juice
  ¼ teaspoon hot pepper sauce
  ⅛ teaspoon ground ancho chiles
  ⅛ teaspoon ground guajillo chiles
  ⅛ teaspoon ground cumin
  ⅛ teaspoon ground Mexican oregano
  ⅛ teaspoon Hungarian paprika
  ⅛ teaspoon Spanish paprika
  ⅛ teaspoon onion salt
  ⅛ teaspoon garlic salt
  ⅛ teaspoon freshly ground black pepper
  ⅛ teaspoon ground white pepper
  ⅛ teaspoon red pepper flakes

  6 half-slabs (14 ounces each) pork ribs, skin
    on underside stripped off
  6 teaspoons Angel Dust Cajun Seasoning
    (page 137)

Combine all ingredients for the sauce in a 3-quart saucepan. Bring to a boil over medium heat. Reduce the heat to low and simmer for 5 minutes, whisking occasionally. Cool and refrigerate until ready to use.

Rub Cajun seasoning all over both sides of the ribs. Place in a dish, to marinate, cover with plastic wrap, and refrigerate for 24 to 48 hours.

When ready to cook, bring the ribs to room temperature and reheat 2 cups of the barbecue sauce. Preheat the oven to 425°. Line two jelly roll pans with aluminum foil and spray lightly with nonstick vegetable spray. Place 3 half-slabs of ribs, meaty side up, on each of the prepared pans and brown in the oven for 25 minutes. Turn ribs over, rotate the pans from the top to the bottom shelf and vice versa, and brown 5 minutes. Remove the ribs from the oven and reduce the oven temperature to 300°. Baste each slab of ribs with 1½ to 2 tablespoons of the BBQ sauce and return to the oven. Continue to cook for 2¼ to 2½ hours until the meat is tender, turning the ribs over and basting frequently with more sauce. To ensure even browning, occasionally rotate the pans during cooking.

Serve with extra sauce.

GRILLED VEAL CHOP
with Veal Reduction and Roasted-Poblano Bread Pudding

SERVES 4

I love a good veal chop, what can I say? This one's pretty straightforward (as the best veal chops tend to be).

Roasted-Poblano Bread Pudding

3 cups (¾-inch cubed) day-old challah bread or any rich egg bread

¼ cup grated Asiago cheese

¼ cup grated Parmesan cheese

2 medium poblano chiles, roasted (see Roasted Peppers, page 142)

2 large eggs

1 cup heavy whipping cream

2 tablespoons honey

1 teaspoon Roasted-Garlic Purée (page 142)

½ teaspoon Worcestershire sauce

½ teaspoon hot pepper sauce

¼ teaspoon freshly ground black pepper

⅛ teaspoon kosher salt

Hot water

Veal Reduction

3 cups Veal Stock (page 140)

Pinch of freshly freshly ground black pepper

Pinch of kosher salt

4 (13 to 14-ounce) veal rib chops

1 teaspoon Angel Dust Cajun Seasoning (page 137)

½ teaspoon freshly ground black pepper

½ teaspoon kosher salt

1 tablespoon extra virgin olive oil

To make the bread pudding, place the bread cubes in a bowl and mix in the cheeses. Peel, seed, and dice the roasted chiles and distribute among the bread cubes. Beat the eggs in a separate bowl. Add the cream, honey, garlic purée, Worcestershire sauce, hot pepper sauce, pepper, and salt, and thoroughly combine. Pour the custard over the bread and allow to soak for 30 minutes, until bread cubes are no longer dry in the center. Mix once or twice while bread is soaking.

Preheat the oven to 350°. Butter an 8½ by 4½-inch loaf pan and pour in the bread-custard mixture. Place the loaf pan in a larger baking pan and transfer to the oven. Carefully pour the hot water into the baking pan until it comes halfway up the sides of the loaf pan. Bake 50 to 55 minutes, until center is set and the inserted tip of a knife comes out clean. Cool until the loaf pan can be carefully removed from the pan holding the hot water.

To prepare the veal reduction, bring the stock to a boil over high heat. Continue to boil for 25 minutes, or until the stock is reduced by two-thirds. Season with pepper and salt.

Heat a charcoal or gas grill. Season the veal chops with the Cajun seasoning, pepper, and salt. Drizzle with the oil, place on the hottest area of the grill, and cook for 5 minutes. Flip over and cook, about 4 minutes, until the chops are nicely browned. Move the chops to the outer edges of the grill where the heat is less intense, and finish cooking, 6 to 7 minutes longer for medium-cooked veal chops.

Reheat the bread pudding and reduction, if necessary. Serve the veal chop and bread pudding with a drizzling of the veal reduction.

GRILLED FILET MIGNON
with Chipotle Black Pepper Sauce

SERVES 4

This pepper sauce on these beef filets reminds me of smoky ketchup with a kick. Much of the smoke and heat is the work of chipotles. As for the mashed potatoes (our recipe's on page 108), one day we just kept adding things we wanted till this is what we had. You can call these potatoes whatever you want, but you won't be able to stop eating them.

Chipotle Black Pepper Sauce
    1 tablespoon extra virgin olive oil
    2 tablespoons finely chopped shallots
    1 teaspoon mashed chipotle chile in
        adobo sauce
    ½ teaspoon Roasted-Garlic Purée
        (page 142)
    ½ teaspoon fresh thyme leaves
    ½ teaspoon chopped fresh rosemary
    ¼ teaspoon Worcestershire sauce
    ⅛ teaspoon coarsely cracked black pepper
    1 small bay leaf
    ½ cup dry red wine, such as Cabernet
        Sauvignon
    2 cups Veal Stock (page 140)
    ¼ teaspoon kosher salt
    1¼ teaspoon cornstarch, mixed with
        1½ teaspoons water
    2 tablespoons unsalted butter, chilled and
        cut into several pieces

    4 (10-ounce) filet mignons
    1 teaspoon Angel Dust Cajun Seasoning
        (page 137)
    ½ teaspoon freshly ground black pepper
    ½ teaspoon kosher salt
    1 tablespoon extra virgin olive oil

Tasso–Corn–Cheddar Cheese–Green Onion
Mashed Potatoes (page 108)

To prepare the sauce, heat the oil in a medium saucepan over medium heat and cook the shallots until soft, about 2 minutes. Add the chipotle pepper, garlic purée, thyme, rosemary, Worcestershire sauce, pepper, and bay leaf, stirring to coat the shallots. Pour in the wine and bring to a boil. Reduce for 12 to 13 minutes, until only a tablespoon of the wine remains. Add the stock and salt, bring to a boil, and continue cooking for 6 minutes, until stock is reduced by one-third.

Whisk in the cornstarch mixture and simmer for 2 to 3 more minutes. Remove the bay leaf. Transfer the sauce to a blender and cover it with the lid. (To prevent hot liquid from splashing out of the blender, cover the lid with a folded dish towel.) On low speed, pulse on and off several times. Purée the sauce until smooth. Strain back into the saucepan through a fine-mesh strainer and whisk in the butter. Set aside.

Heat a charcoal or gas grill. Season the filets with the Cajun seasoning, pepper, and salt, and drizzle with the oil. Place on the hottest area of the grill and cook for 5 minutes. Flip over and cook until the steaks are nicely browned, about 5 minutes. Move the filets to the outer edges of the grill where the heat is less intense and finish cooking, 6 to 10 minutes for medium-cooked steaks.

Reheat the sauce, if necessary, and serve drizzled over the filets and the mashed potatoes.

STEAK PO-BOY
with Grilled Bell Peppers and Onions

SERVES 4

Why not put great beef on a po-boy? It may not be "poor" anymore, but it's still great. With New York strip, Creole seasoning and Worcestershire, this is my upgrade on Italian sausage and peppers. Street food it ain't.

Garlic-Butter Spread (page 83)

4 (6-inch) deli-style or hoagie rolls, split lengthwise

4 (6-ounce) thin, boneless, strip steaks, trimmed

½ teaspoon Angel Dust Cajun Seasoning (page 137)

¼ teaspoon salt

¼ teaspoon freshly ground black pepper

2 teaspoons plus 2 teaspoons olive oil

1 large green bell pepper, seeded and cut into quarters

1 large red bell pepper, seeded and cut into quarters

4 (⅜-inch thick) slices sweet yellow onion

4 slices cheese, such as Muenster, provolone, or smoked Gouda (optional)

Spread the cut side of each roll with the garlic butter. Set aside on a heat-proof tray, such as a jelly roll pan.

Season the steaks on both sides with the Cajun seasoning, salt, and pepper, then drizzle with 2 teaspoons of the oil. Drizzle the bell peppers and onions with the remaining 2 teaspoons oil.

When ready to cook, heat a charcoal or gas grill. Begin grilling the peppers over high heat for 3 minutes. Add the onions, grilling both peppers and onions for 5 more minutes, turning occasionally. While the vegetables are cooking, grill the buttered side of the rolls for 1 to 1½ minutes. Flip the rolls over and grill the outside for 30 seconds. Transfer the rolls to the tray.

Transfer the peppers and onions to a plate and cover with aluminum foil. Grill the steaks for 3 minutes, turn over, and grill for 2 more minutes. Place cheese on the cooking steaks and allow the cheese to melt. This should take 45 seconds to 1 minute. Transfer a steak to each roll, break up the rings of the grilled onion slices, and place on each steak. Cut each bell pepper slice into several strips and distribute evenly among the sandwiches. Serve immediately.

SIDE DISHES

CORN BREAD

SERVES 6 TO 8

I always make my corn bread moist and sweet, like cake. On the other hand, I almost always make it with jalapeños and cheddar cheese, an option here. If you aren't able to serve this hot out of the oven, experiment with reheating for a few seconds in the microwave. The cheese tastes lots better when it's bubbly.

1⅓ cups all-purpose flour
1 cup plus 2 tablespoons finely ground corn flour (see note)
⅔ cup granulated sugar
5 teaspoons baking powder
½ teaspoon kosher salt
1 large egg
1⅓ cups milk
5 tablespoons unsalted butter, melted
1 teaspoon bacon drippings, optional

Preheat the oven to 350°. Grease an 8 by 8-inch baking pan. Combine the flours, sugar, baking powder, and salt in a large bowl. In a small bowl, lightly beat the egg, then whisk in the milk, butter, and bacon drippings. Pour the wet ingredients into the flour mixture and mix until smooth. Transfer to the prepared pan and bake 50 minutes, until golden brown. Cool slightly before cutting.

Cheddar-Jalapeño Corn Bread
For variety, fold 1 cup grated cheddar cheese and 3 tablespoons seeded, chopped jalapeño into the batter after combining the wet and dry ingredients.

Note
Corn flour is available in some grocery stores with ethnic-food sections.

PICO DE GALLO SALSA

MAKES 2 CUPS

2 cups (about 4 medium) diced plum tomatoes
3 tablespoons finely chopped red onion
1 tablespoon minced fresh cilantro
2 teaspoons seeded, minced jalapeño
1 teaspoon freshly squeezed lemon juice
½ teaspoon salt
⅛ teaspoon ground white pepper

Combine the salsa ingredients in a small bowl, cover, and refrigerate until needed for up to 3 days.

ROASTED-GARLIC MASHED POTATOES

SERVES 4

These mashed potatoes are a signature dish at Heaven on Seven. Yukon Gold potatoes are wonderful all alone. But wait till you taste them with heavy cream and garlic. Try them at your next Sunday dinner. They won't last five minutes.

1½ pounds small Yukon Gold potatoes
1 cup heavy whipping cream
4 tablespoons unsalted butter
1 tablespoon Roasted-Garlic Purée
  (page 142)
¾ teaspoon kosher salt
⅛ teaspoon ground white pepper

Scrub potatoes. Boil in salted water for 30 minutes. Drain. Cool slightly until potatoes can be handled comfortably, then peel and transfer to a large bowl. In a small saucepan, heat the cream, butter, and garlic purée until mixture just comes to a boil. Pour over the potatoes while mashing with a potato masher. Season with salt and pepper. Serve immediately.

Note
Boiling potatoes with their skin on keeps lots of wonderful flavor in.

ROASTED-POBLANO MASHED POTATOES

SERVES 4

Start with roasted-garlic mashed potatoes and add some roasted poblanos for heat. Don't overdo the chiles, though (I bet you thought you'd never hear me say that!). You want to be able to taste the potatoes.

1½ pounds small Yukon Gold potatoes
1 cup heavy cream
4 tablespoons unsalted butter
1 tablespoon Roasted-Garlic Purée
  (page 142)
¾ teaspoon kosher salt
⅛ teaspoon ground white pepper

1 large roasted poblano chile (page 142),
  seeded and finely diced

Scrub potatoes. Boil in salted water for 30 minutes. Drain. Cool slightly until potatoes can be handled comfortably, then peel and transfer to a large bowl. In a small saucepan, heat the cream, butter, and garlic purée until mixture just comes to a boil. Pour over the potatoes while mashing with a potato masher. Mix in the poblano chile and season with salt and pepper. Serve immediately.

Tasso–Corn–Cheddar Cheese– Green Onion Mashed Potatoes

SERVES 4

These are mashed potatoes that got out of hand. The good news is that they taste so good, nobody wants to stop them from getting out of hand again and again.

1¼ pounds Yukon Gold potatoes
2 tablespoons unsalted butter
¼ cup diced tasso ham
¼ cup thinly sliced green onion, white and green parts
½ cup fresh or frozen corn kernels
1 teaspoon Roasted-Garlic Purée (page 142)
¾ cup heavy whipping cream
⅓ cup grated Cheddar cheese
¼ teaspoon kosher salt
Pinch of ground white pepper

Scrub potatoes. Boil in salted water for 30 minutes. Drain. Cool slightly until potatoes can be handled comfortably, then peel and transfer to a large bowl. While potatoes are cooking, melt the butter in a small sauté pan over medium heat. Add the ham and onions and sauté for 1 minute. Mix in the corn and garlic, and cook, stirring, for an additional minute. Reduce the heat to low, cook for 4 minutes, and set aside. In a small saucepan, heat the cream until mixture just comes to a boil. Remove from the heat and stir in the cheese until melted. Pour over the potatoes while mashing with a potato masher. Mix in the ham and vegetables and season with salt and pepper. Serve immediately.

White Rice

MAKES 3 CUPS

3 cups hot tap water
1 cup converted white rice

Bring the hot water and rice to a boil in a 3-quart saucepan over high heat. Cover and continue boiling for 20 to 22 minutes. Test rice for doneness. Rinse under hot water and drain.

COLLARD GREENS

SERVES 8

I've always loved collard greens, but it wasn't until a longtime customer shared a secret family recipe that I grew to adore them. The Italian dressing was the recipe's idea; the brown sugar was mine—a neat way to smooth out the vinegar. In my restaurants, I am always surprised to see how many different kinds of people order collard greens—and I assume they're not all Southerners by birth. Construction workers, doctors, lawyers, plumbers, developers, and politicians—all eat serious greens with their sleeves rolled up.

4 pounds fresh collard greens
2 tablespoons extra virgin olive oil
1½ cups diced yellow onion
2 tablespoons Roasted-Garlic Purée
   (page 142)
1 tablespoon seeded, minced jalapeño
1 cup shredded pickled pork or Shredded
   Smoked Pork Shoulder Butt (page 141)
½ cup diced tasso ham
2 tablespoons distilled white vinegar
1 tablespoon granulated sugar
1 tablespoon light brown sugar
1 tablespoon dark brown sugar
¼ teaspoon Angel Dust Cajun Seasoning
   (page 137)
¼ teaspoon kosher salt
¼ teaspoon crushed red pepper flakes
⅛ teaspoon freshly ground black pepper
⅛ teaspoon ground white pepper
3 cups water
1 cup bottled Italian dressing

Wash the collard greens several times in a large quantity of water; drain well. Pull the thick center core out of each leaf and discard; tear leaves into medium-sized pieces. Heat the oil in a large Dutch oven over high heat; sauté the onions until soft, about 3 minutes. Add the garlic purée and jalapeño and cook another minute. Add the pork and ham, and brown for 3 minutes. Mix in the vinegar, sugars, Cajun seasoning, salt, red pepper flakes, and ground black and white peppers, stirring to coat the onions and meat. Add the greens, water, and dressing to the pot. Toss the greens as they begin to cook down and the liquid comes to a boil. Cover and reduce the heat to medium-low and simmer for 1 hour and 25 minutes.

Note

Make sure to serve plenty of corn bread with the greens to soak up the vitamin-rich "pot likker" released from the greens.

PARMESAN CHEESE GRITS

SERVES 4

I can't think of grits without thinking of polenta, so it's natural for me to build up this quirky Deep South favorite with butter, heavy cream, and Parmesan. Wow! These grits are wonderful with eggs, a piece of steak, or any type of seafood. Especially in Chicago, polenta has helped grits get some respect.

1½ cups heavy whipping cream
½ cup water
2 tablespoons unsalted butter
½ teaspoon Roasted-Garlic Purée
   (page 142)
⅛ teaspoon kosher salt
⅛ teaspoon white pepper
¼ cup quick-cooking grits
⅓ cup grated Parmesan cheese
2 tablespoons grated Asiago cheese

In a 3-quart saucepan, bring cream, water, butter, garlic purée, salt, and pepper to a boil over medium heat. Slowly add grits, whisking continuously until incorporated. Turn heat to low and cook, whisking frequently, for 25 minutes. Add the cheese and cook, stirring, for 5 more minutes.

ANDOUILLE POLENTA

SERVES 4

I'm a soft-polenta guy, so I don't like all those triangles and squares of hard grilled polenta that many restaurants offer up. For me, polenta should be flowing and smooth. It's quite all right, though, if it hooks up with Cajun sausage for a little smoke and heat.

2 tablespoons unsalted butter
4 ounces andouille sausage, cut into ¼-inch
   slices and chopped
1 tablespoon minced yellow onion
1⅓ cups heavy whipping cream
¼ teaspoon Roasted-Garlic Purée
   (page 142)
⅛ teaspoon Angel Dust Cajun Seasoning
   (page 137)
¼ cup instant polenta

Melt the butter over medium heat in a 3-quart saucepan. Sauté the andouille for 3 minutes. Add the onion and sauté for 2 minutes. Add the cream, garlic purée, and Cajun seasoning, and bring to a boil. Slowly whisk in the polenta. Reduce the heat to low and continue cooking for 7 minutes, stirring continuously.

CAJUN COLESLAW

SERVES 4

My honey-jalapeño dressing is the only secret to making the creamiest coleslaw you'll ever taste. It's sweet, with just the right amount of jalapeño bite.

1 pound shredded green cabbage (see note)
⅓ cup thinly sliced green onion,
    white and green parts
¼ cup shredded carrots

Honey-Jalapeño Dressing
⅔ cup mayonnaise
½ cup heavy whipping cream
2 tablespoons honey
5 teaspoons granulated sugar
1½ teaspoons seeded, minced jalapeño
½ teaspoon kosher salt
¼ teaspoon Angel Dust Cajun Seasoning
    (page 137)
¼ teaspoon Worcestershire sauce
¼ teaspoon hot pepper sauce
¼ teaspoon ground white pepper
⅛ teaspoon freshly ground black pepper
⅛ teaspoon ground cayenne

Combine the cabbage, onion, and carrots in a medium-sized bowl and set aside.

To make the dressing, whisk all the ingredients together until combined. Pour over the cabbage and mix thoroughly. Cover and refrigerate for at least 1 hour, or until ready to serve.

Note
Packaged coleslaw mix would work fine here as a substitute for the cabbage.

DESSERTS

SWEET POTATO PIE

The sweet potato pie created by Omar the Pie Man inspired this dessert. I first tasted his pie at Jazzfest in New Orleans. His version was fried. Mine is baked, but it has the same level of creamy sweetness that Omar's had. Since so many of my customers come to this by way of pumpkin pie, we keep the spice profile in the same ballpark.

Basic Pie Dough

- 7 tablespoons unsalted butter, at room temperature
- 2 teaspoons granulated sugar
- ¼ teaspoon salt
- 1 large egg
- 1½ cups all-purpose flour
- 2 tablespoons ice water

Filling

- 2 large sweet potatoes, 1 pound each
- 3 tablespoons unsalted butter, at room temperature
- 2 large eggs
- 2 large egg yolks
- ½ cup granulated sugar
- ½ cup light brown sugar
- 2 teaspoons pure vanilla extract
- ¼ teaspoon salt
- ¼ teaspoon ground nutmeg
- ¾ cup heavy whipping cream
- 1 teaspoon bourbon

To make the pie dough, beat together the butter, sugar, and salt for 3 minutes on medium speed in the bowl of an electric mixer. Add the egg and beat for 30 seconds. Add the flour and water and beat for 15 seconds. Turn off the machine, scrape down the sides of the bowl, and beat again for 10 seconds. Scoop up the dough with your hands and form it into a 1-inch thick disk. Wrap in plastic wrap and refrigerate for at least 1 hour.

Preheat the oven to 400° degrees. Place the potatoes on a baking sheet and roast for 50 minutes. Cool for 10 minutes, peel, and cut into several pieces. Transfer the warm potatoes and the butter to the bowl of a food processor and process until smooth. Beat the eggs, egg yolks, sugars, vanilla, salt, and nutmeg in the bowl of an electric mixer on low for 3 minutes.

Mix in the cream. Add the puréed sweet potatoes and bourbon; beat for 1 minute. Stop the machine and scrape down the sides of the bowl; beat again until ingredients are incorporated, about 20 seconds.

Heat the oven to 350°. On a lightly floured surface, roll out the pie dough into a 12-inch circle, to a fit a 10-inch deep-dish pie plate. Transfer the dough to the plate; trim any excess and crimp the edges. Pour the sweet potato filling into the shell, transfer to a baking sheet, and bake for 1 hour, or until center is set. Chill in the refrigerator for several hours before serving.

CHOCOLATE PECAN PIE

It's pretty hard to make Southern pecan pie any better than it is, except by adding chocolate. I see this as the best of two worlds.

Basic Pie Dough (page 114)

Filling

5 ounces semisweet chocolate chips or
   finely chopped chocolate pieces
6 tablespoons unsalted butter, cut into
   several pieces
1 tablespoon pure vanilla extract
4 large eggs
1¾ cups granulated sugar
1 cup dark corn syrup
1½ cups pecan halves
Whipped cream or ice cream
Vanilla Bean Caramel Sauce (page 130)
Chocolate Sauce (page 131)

On a lightly floured surface, roll out the pie dough into a 12-inch circle to fit a 10-inch deep-dish pie plate. Transfer the dough to the plate; trim any excess, and crimp the edges. Refrigerate for 30 minutes before preparing the filling.

Preheat the oven to 325°. Bring water to a simmer in the bottom of a double boiler, then lower the heat to the lowest possible setting. Place the chocolate and butter in the top of the double boiler and whisk until melted. Whisk in the vanilla and the eggs, one at a time. Whisk in the sugar and beat with a whisk for 2 minutes, until the sugar is almost completely dissolved. Add the corn syrup and continue beating until completely incorporated. Remove the pie plate from the refrigerator and spread the pecans on the bottom of the dough. Pour in the chocolate mixture.

Place the pie on a baking sheet, transfer to the oven, and bake for 30 minutes. Reduce the temperature to 275° and continue baking for 50 minutes. Allow to cool for 2 hours, then refrigerate for 45 minutes before cutting. (During baking, the pecans will rise to the surface. The filling will puff slightly but will settle back down upon cooling.) If refrigerating overnight, let pie come to room temperature before serving.

Serve with whipped cream or ice cream and a drizzling of caramel and chocolate sauce.

FRIED PEACH PIE

SERVES 6

Remember Omar the Pie Man in New Orleans, the guy who taught me about sweet potato pie? Well, his tendency to fry anything in dough sounded just right for peaches. If you've ever made a Latin empanada or a Caribbean patty, you'll feel right at home with this recipe.

Sweet Pie Dough

8 tablespoons unsalted butter, at room
    temperature
1½ tablespoons granulated sugar
¼ teaspoon salt
1 large egg
1½ cups all-purpose flour
2 tablespoons ice water
1 tablespoon unsalted butter

1 pound frozen peaches, thawed, or
    2 cups sliced fresh peaches
1½ tablespoons granulated sugar
¼ cup peach jam or preserves
Pinch of ground cayenne pepper
Pinch of ground white pepper
Vegetable oil for deep frying

To prepare the pie dough, beat together the butter, sugar, and salt for 3 minutes on medium speed in the bowl of an electric mixer. Add the egg and beat for 30 seconds. Add the flour and water and beat for 15 seconds. Turn off the machine, scrape down the sides of the bowl, and beat again for 10 seconds. Scoop up the dough with your hands and form it into a 1-inch thick disk. Wrap in plastic wrap and refrigerate for at least 1 hour.

Melt the butter over medium-high heat in a medium-sized sauté pan. Sauté the peaches and sugar until the sugar is dissolved, about 2 minutes. Add the jam or preserves, cayenne, and white pepper; cook, stirring frequently, for 3 minutes. Cool for 10 minutes.

On a lightly floured surface, roll out the dough into a 16 by 11-inch rectangle about ⅛ inch thick. Cut out six 5¼-inch circles. (For a more free-form shape, divide the dough into six pieces and roll out.) Place the circles on a baking sheet lined with parchment or wax paper. Fill the lower half of each circle with about ¼ cup of the cooked peaches. Fold the top half of the dough over the filling and crimp the edges securely with a fork. Refrigerate for 20 minutes before frying.

Heat 2½ inches of vegetable oil to 350° in a heavy 4-quart saucepan. Fry pies 2 or 3 at a time until golden brown, 1½ to 2 minutes per batch. Drain on paper towels. Keep warm in a 200° oven until all the pies are fried. Serve immediately with ice cream.

KEY LIME ICEBOX PIE

Everybody loves Key lime pie, but I was looking for something a little better. What turned out a little better was putting lime curd on the bottom and lime chiffon on the top. The cool lime taste makes a perfect finale for a highly seasoned dinner.

Graham Cracker Crust (page 121)

Key Lime Curd

½ teaspoon granulated gelatin
1 tablespoon cold water
¼ cup freshly squeezed Key lime juice
1 cup heavy whipping cream
⅓ cup granulated sugar
4 large egg yolks
Pinch of salt
3 tablespoons unsalted butter, chilled
   and cut into pieces

Key Lime Chiffon

1 teaspoon granulated gelatin
2 tablespoons cold water
6 tablespoons freshly squeezed
   Key lime juice
2 large egg yolks
½ cup plus 3 tablespoons granulated sugar
2 large egg whites
1½ cups heavy whipping cream

To prepare the lime curd, soak gelatin in the cold water for 3 to 5 minutes, until it softens. While gelatin is soaking, heat the Key lime juice to a boil in a small saucepan or in a glass measuring cup in the microwave. Dissolve the gelatin in the hot juice. Keep warm.

Combine the cream, sugar, egg yolks, and salt in a medium-sized saucepan. Whisk over medium heat until the sugar is dissolved, about 2 minutes. Reduce the heat to medium-low, stirring continuously and scraping up the cooked custard mixture as it begins to thicken, about 6 minutes more. Slowly pour the warm lime juice and gelatin mixture into the hot custard while whisking continuously until the the gelatin is completely dissolved. Remove from the heat and gradually whisk in the butter until melted. Set aside to cool for 20 minutes. Pour into the prepared graham cracker crust spreading evenly along the bottom of the crust and refrigerate until set, about 2 hours.

To prepare the lime chiffon, soak the gelatin in the cold water in a small heatproof bowl for 3 to 5 minutes. Heat the lime juice to a boil in a medium saucepan, then pour into the bowl containing the softened gelatin, whisking until the gelatin is dissolved in the hot juice. In the saucepan used to heat the lime juice, thoroughly combine the egg yolks and ½ cup sugar. Slowly whisk in the warm lime juice and gelatin mixture. Turn the heat to medium-low and whisk the mixture until frothy and the sugar is dissolved, about 3 minutes. Transfer the mixture to the bowl of an electric mixer and whip on medium speed until thick and fluffy, about 5 minutes. Transfer to a large bowl.

In a separate bowl, whip egg whites until soft, about 2 minutes; then beat in 2 tablespoons of the remaining sugar until medium-stiff peaks form, about 2 minutes. Fold half of the beaten egg whites into the cooled lime mixture; then fold in the other half. Quickly whip the cream along with the remaining 1 tablespoon of sugar until medium-stiff peaks form. Fold into the lime-egg white mixture. Mound the chiffon on top of the chilled lime curd and spread over the entire pie top. Refrigerate until set, at least 6 hours or overnight.

Note

This method gets the egg yolk temperature up to 160°, so only the whites remain uncooked.

If you can't get fresh Key limes, go ahead and use bottled juice.

CHOCOLATE–PEANUT BUTTER PIE

SERVES10

As ET understood, chocolate and peanut butter are a marriage made in heaven. You'll be even more certain that's true once you've sampled this pie filling in a graham cracker crust. Be sure to whip the cream-cheese-and-peanut-butter filling until it's light and airy.

Graham Cracker Crust

1½ cups graham cracker crumbs
3 tablespoons light brown sugar
5 tablespoons unsalted butter, melted

Filling

8 ounces cream cheese, at room
   temperature
¾ cup granulated sugar
½ cup light brown sugar
2 teaspoons pure vanilla extract
¼ teaspoon salt
1 cup creamy peanut butter
1 cup heavy whipping cream

Ganache

3 ounces bittersweet chocolate chips or
   finely chopped chocolate pieces
½ cup heavy whipping cream
Vanilla Bean Caramel Sauce (page 130)

Preheat the oven to 325°. To prepare the crust, combine the graham cracker crumbs and brown sugar in the bowl of an electric mixer on low speed. With the mixer running, add the butter and mix until just combined. Transfer to a 10-inch deep-dish pie plate. Press the crumb mixture onto the sides and bottom of the pie plate. Bake for 10 minutes. Remove from the oven and allow to cool.

Beat the cream cheese in the bowl of an electric mixer until fluffy, about 2 minutes. Add the granulated and brown sugars, vanilla, and salt, and beat until smooth, about 5 minutes. Scrape down the sides of the bowl, add the peanut butter, and continue beating until peanut butter is incorporated, 1 to 2 minutes more. Set aside. In another bowl, whip the cream to the soft peak stage and fold into the cream-cheese-and-peanut-butter mixture.

Pour into the prepared pie crust and refrigerate for 2 hours.

While pie is chilling, make the ganache. Place the chocolate in a small heatproof bowl. In a small saucepan, heat the cream just to a boil and pour over the chocolate. Let rest for 3 to 4 minutes, or until chocolate melts. Whisk until mixture is smooth. Set aside to cool. The ganache topping should be warm enough to pour easily onto the pie but cool enough not to melt it. Pour the ganache onto the pie; either spread it to the edges with a spatula, or hold the pie in your hands and rotate it, allowing the chocolate to coat the entire top. Refrigerate until the ganache is set.

Serve with a drizzling of caramel sauce.

COCONUT-CREAM CAKE

SERVES 12

Nobody I know seems to eat cake anymore. But cakes always remind me of Sunday church socials in the South, where people's generosity can be found in the foods they serve. Those thoughts inspired this cake. With its toasted coconut, it's sweet, chunky, and nutty all at the same time. Amen!

Coconut-Cream Filling

1 (15-ounce) can unsweetened coconut milk
5 teaspoons cornstarch
½ cup half-and-half
¼ cup plus ¼ cup granulated sugar
Pinch of salt
4 large egg yolks
½ teaspoon pure vanilla extract
1 tablespoon unsalted butter
½ cup toasted coconut (page 66)

Layer Cake

3½ cups all-purpose flour
2½ teaspoons baking powder
2½ teaspoons baking soda
¼ teaspoon salt
1 pound unsalted butter, softened
2½ cups granulated sugar
7 large egg yolks
1 tablespoon pure vanilla extract
1¾ cups milk
7 large egg whites
¼ teaspoon cream of tartar

Fluffy Frosting

4 ounces unsalted butter, at room temperature
4 ounces cream cheese, at room temperature

3 cups confectioners' sugar
3 tablespoons heavy whipping cream
2 teaspoons pure vanilla extract
Pinch of salt
1½ cups toasted coconut (refer to page 66)

Coconut Crème Anglaise (page 129)
Vanilla Bean Caramel Sauce (page 130)

To prepare the filling, mix 3 tablespoons of the coconut milk with the cornstarch. Set aside. In a medium-sized saucepan, bring the remaining coconut milk, half-and-half, ¼ cup sugar, and salt to a simmer over medium-high heat, stirring for 2 minutes or until sugar is dissolved. Whisk together the egg yolks, ¼ cup sugar, and vanilla in a medium bowl; slowly pour in the coconut-milk mixture, whisking continuously.

Return the liquid to the saucepan; whisk continuously while the cream simmers over low heat and until it begins to thicken, about 5 minutes. Whisk in the cornstarch mixture, cook for 2 minutes, then add the butter and stir until melted. Remove from the heat and blend in the toasted coconut. Transfer to a bowl and lay a piece of plastic wrap on top of the cream filling to prevent a skin from accumulating on the surface. Refrigerate for at least 2 hours, or until set.

Preheat the oven to 350°. Butter and flour three 10-inch cake pans. Sift the flour, baking powder, baking soda, and salt together; set aside. In the bowl of an electric mixer, beat the butter on medium speed for 1 minute. Add the sugar, and the egg yolks one at a time, beating after each addition. Add the vanilla and beat until mixture is fluffy, about 3 minutes. Lower the speed and mix in half the dry ingredients. Add the milk, then the remaining dry ingredients.

In a separate bowl, whip the egg whites with the cream of tartar until soft peaks form. Fold some of the whites into the cake batter to loosen up the batter and prevent the whites from breaking down. Add the remaining whites, folding in gently until incorporated. Divide batter among the three prepared pans and bake for 20 minutes, or until a skewer inserted into the cake comes out clean. Cool.

To assemble the cake, place one layer on a plate and spread with half of the coconut-cream filling. Place the second layer on top of the filling and spread with the remaining filling. Place the third layer on top.

To make the frosting, beat together the butter and cream cheese in the bowl of an electric mixer until smooth. On low speed, add the confectioners' sugar, cream, vanilla, and salt, and beat for 1 minute. Increase the speed to high and beat until fluffy, about 2 minutes. Immediately spread the frosting in a thin layer on the top and sides of the cake. Press the toasted coconut all over into the frosting.

Serve with the crème anglaise and a drizzling of caramel sauce.

BOURBON STREET FLOURLESS CHOCOLATE CAKE

SERVES 10

This recipe is by Chef Paulie Papadopoulos at the Rush Street Restaurant. It's a chocoholic's dream, very dense and very intense.

8 ounces unsalted butter
4 ounces bittersweet chocolate chips or
    coarsely chopped chocolate pieces
½ cup water
⅓ cup sugar
6 large eggs
Hot water

Glaze
4 ounces bittersweet chocolate chips or
    finely chopped chocolate pieces
½ cup heavy whipping cream
Bourbon Crème Anglaise (see variation of
    Crème Anglaise, page 128)

Bring water to a simmer in the bottom of a double boiler, then lower the heat to the lowest possible setting. Place the chocolate and butter in the top of the double boiler and whisk until melted. Remove from the heat and allow the melted chocolate mixture to cool.

In a small saucepan, stir together the water and sugar. Bring the mixture to a boil over medium-high heat; simmer until the sugar is dissolved, about 1 minute. Cool the sugar syrup for 20 minutes.

Preheat the oven to 300°. Bring a pot of water to a boil while preparing the cake.

Lightly beat the eggs in a medium-sized bowl. Slowly add the cooled sugar syrup, whisking continuously. Mix in the melted chocolate and butter mixture. Pour batter into a 9-inch straight-sided cake pan. Place cake pan in a large baking pan and transfer to the oven. Carefully pour hot water halfway up the sides of the cake pan and bake for 30 minutes.

Cool cake completely in its pan. Wrap with plastic wrap and refrigerate at least 1 hour.

While the cake is cooling, make the glaze. Place the chocolate in a small bowl. Scald the cream and pour over the chocolate. Let sit for 3 to 4 minutes, then stir until all the chocolate is melted. Cool for 1 hour.

To unmold the cake, place a plate over the cake pan and invert it; tap gently to release the cake. With another plate, flip the cake over again so the top of the cake is facing up. Pour the glaze over the cake, spreading it evenly with a spatula. Refrigerate until completely chilled.

Serve with the crème anglaise.

Note
This cake is only an inch or so high, but very rich. Cut into thin wedges for serving.

BREAD PUDDING

On the wall on Wabash Street, there's a newspaper clipping showcasing my late mother and her terrific bread pudding, a dessert that helped put Heaven on Seven on the map. This is her recipe. Interestingly, we serve it cold on Wabash but hot on Rush. I can assure you that you'll love it either way.

1 cup golden raisins
¼ cup bourbon
16 cups (¾-inch cubed) day-old challah or
   any rich egg bread
4 ounces (1 stick) unsalted butter, melted
½ cup plus 1 cup granulated sugar
1 teaspoon plus 1 teaspoon ground
   cinnamon
4½ cups heavy whipping cream
1 tablespoon pure vanilla extract
½ teaspoon ground nutmeg
8 large eggs
Hot water
Vanilla Bean Caramel Sauce (page 130)

In a small bowl, soak the raisins in the bourbon.

Place the bread cubes in a large bowl and drizzle the butter over them. Mix the ½ cup sugar and 1 teaspoon cinnamon together and sprinkle over the bread, tossing to distribute evenly. Heat the cream, 1 cup sugar, vanilla, nutmeg, and remaining teaspoon of cinnamon over low heat, stirring until the sugar is dissolved, about 2 minutes. Do not boil. Place the eggs in a bowl and slowly whisk in the warm cream. Pour the cream over the bread, mix in the raisins, and allow to stand for 45 minutes to 1 hour, until bread cubes are no longer dry in the center. Mix once or twice during standing.

Preheat the oven to 350°. Butter a 9 by 13-inch glass baking dish and pour in the bread mixture. Place the dish in a larger baking pan and transfer to the oven. Carefully pour hot water into the baking pan until it comes halfway up the sides of the dish. Bake 55 to 60 minutes, or until center is set and the inserted tip of a knife comes out clean. Remove from oven and cool until the dish can be safely removed from the pan holding the hot water.

Serve warm with the caramel sauce.

CHOCOLATE BREAD PUDDING

SERVES 10

Taking a good thing and making it better is what gets us going each morning at Heaven on Seven. And that's what we do here with my mother's bread pudding recipe. A little bit of chocolate makes a big difference.

16 cups (¾-inch cubed) day-old challah or any rich egg bread
3 cups half-and-half
1½ cups heavy whipping cream
1¾ cups light brown sugar
2 teaspoons pure vanilla extract
½ teaspoon ground cinnamon
¼ teaspoon ground nutmeg
1½ cups (about 9 ounces) semisweet chocolate chips or finely chopped chocolate pieces
6 large eggs
Chocolate Sauce (page 131)

Place the bread cubes in a large bowl. Heat the half-and-half, cream, sugar, vanilla, cinnamon, and nutmeg in a 3-quart saucepan over low heat, stirring until the sugar is dissolved, 4 to 5 minutes. (The liquid should not boil, but it should be warm enough to melt the chocolate.) Remove from the heat and add the chocolate. Let sit for 4 minutes, then stir until chocolate is melted. Cool for 30 minutes. Place the eggs in a bowl and slowly whisk in the chocolate custard. Pour over the bread and allow to stand for 1 hour, until bread cubes are no longer dry in the center. Mix several times during standing.

Preheat the oven to 350° degrees. Butter a 9 by 13-inch glass baking dish and pour in the bread mixture. Place the dish in a larger baking pan and transfer to the oven. Carefully pour the hot water into the baking pan until it comes halfway up the sides of the dish. Bake for 55 to 60 minutes until center is set and the inserted tip of a knife comes out clean. Remove from the oven and cool until the dish can be safely removed from the pan holding the hot water.

Serve warm with the chocolate sauce.

Chicory Coffee Crème Brûlée

6 SERVINGS

Some of the crème brûlée flavors floating around these days are mighty wacky. But this one makes complete sense to me—it incorporates that ultimate New Orleans flavor of coffee with chicory. Any coffee with chicory or sold as New Orleans blend will work—in this crème brûlée and in the cup you sip with it.

1 quart heavy whipping cream
1 cup plus 3 tablespoons granulated sugar
½ of a vanilla bean, split lengthwise
2½ tablespoons ground chicory coffee
4 teaspoons ground French roast coffee
10 egg yolks
Hot water
6 (8-ounce) heatproof ramekins or custard cups

Heat the oven to 325°. Bring 2 to 3 quarts of water to a boil.

Combine the cream, 1 cup of sugar, and vanilla bean in a medium-sized saucepan. Over medium heat, bring the mixture to just before the boiling point. Remove from the heat, whisk in the coffees, and let the mixture steep for 10 minutes. Strain through a fine mesh strainer. Place the egg yolks in a medium-sized bowl. Whisk a small amount of the hot cream into the eggs a little at a time. Continue adding the cream, whisking continuously, until all the cream is incorporated. Strain again (to remove any egg that may have coagulated).

Place the heatproof ramekins in a large baking pan 2½ to 3 inches deep. Ladle the warm liquid into the ramekins. Transfer the pan to the oven and carefully pour enough hot water into the pan to come halfway up the sides of the ramekins. Bake until custard is set, 1 hour to 1 hour and 15 minutes. Remove from the oven and cool slightly, then carefully remove ramekins from the hot water.

Chill for at least 4 hours. To serve, heat the broiler. Evenly sprinkle the remaining 3 tablespoons sugar on top of the chilled custard. Place the ramekins on the level surface of the broiler pan and broil for 1½ to 2 minutes to caramelize the sugar. Carefully remove from the broiler and let sit for 3 or 4 minutes until the caramelized sugar hardens.

CRÈME ANGLAISE

1⅓ cups heavy whipping cream
⅓ cup granulated sugar
½ of a vanilla bean, split lengthwise
3 large egg yolks

Heat the cream, sugar, and vanilla bean over medium heat, to just before the boiling point. Whisk the egg yolks in a medium-sized bowl. Slowly pour the hot cream into the egg yolks, whisking continuously. Pour the mixture back into the pan and cook over low heat for 4 to 5 minutes, stirring continuously. Do not let the mixture boil. Strain the sauce into a small bowl. Remove the vanilla bean. Scrape out the tiny seeds with the tip of a knife, and whisk into the sauce. Cool and refrigerate in a covered container. Sauce will keep for 4 to 5 days in the refrigerator.

Variation
Stir 1 tablespoon bourbon into the sauce after straining.

Coconut Crème Anglaise

1 cup heavy whipping cream
¾ cup unsweetened coconut milk
½ cup flaked sweetened coconut
¼ cup granulated sugar
3 large egg yolks

Heat the cream, coconut milk, flaked coconut, and sugar over medium heat, to just before the boiling point. Let the mixture steep for 20 minutes. Whisk the egg yolks in a medium-sized bowl. Slowly pour the hot cream into the egg yolks, whisking continuously. Pour the mixture through a fine-mesh strainer back into the pan, pressing out any liquid from the flaked coconut. Discard the flaked coconut.

Cook over low heat for 4 minutes, stirring continuously. Do not let the mixture boil. Strain the sauce again into a small bowl. Cool and refrigerate in a covered container. Sauce will keep for 4 to 5 days in the refrigerator.

Vanilla Bean Caramel Sauce

¾ cup heavy whipping cream
½ of a vanilla bean, split lengthwise
1 cup granulated sugar
3 tablespoons dark corn syrup
4 tablespoons unsalted butter, chilled and
   cut into pieces

Bring the cream and vanilla bean to a boil in a small saucepan over medium heat. Remove from the heat and let steep for 10 minutes. Remove the vanilla bean. Scrape out the tiny seeds with the tip of a knife, and add to the cream. Discard the vanilla bean. Set aside.

Place the sugar and corn syrup in a 3-quart saucepan and, using a wooden spoon, mix until as much of the sugar is coated with the syrup as possible. Scrape any sugar back into the pan. Turn the heat to medium. The sugar will begin to break down after 3 or 4 minutes. Stir once or twice, mixing the undissolved sugar into the warm liquid. When it becomes foamy after about 2 more minutes, stop stirring. Continue heating for 2 minutes until the syrup begins to turn medium brown. Whisk in the butter a little at a time and continue whisking until the mixture comes together. Remove from the heat and very slowly whisk in the cream a little at a time. The caramel is extremely hot and initially will bubble up as the cream is being added. Return the saucepan to the burner over low heat and stir until the caramel sauce is completely smooth and all ingredients are incorporated. Sauce will thicken as it cools. Allow the caramel to cool completely before storing in a covered container in the refrigerator. Serve warm.

CHOCOLATE SAUCE

⅓ cup water

¼ cup granulated sugar

2 tablespoons cocoa powder

½ cup bittersweet chocolate chips or finely
   chopped chocolate pieces

¾ cup heavy whipping cream

Bring the water and sugar to a boil in a medium saucepan over medium-high heat. Whisk in the cocoa powder. Add the chocolate, remove from the heat, and let sit for 3 minutes. Stir the chocolate until it melts; add the cream and incorporate completely. Sauce will thicken as it cools.

Store in a covered container in the refrigerator. Serve at room temperature (it's pretty good straight out of the fridge too!).

BASICS

DARK ROUX

2 cups canola oil
2½ cups all-purpose flour

Heat oil in a 4-quart dutch oven over high heat until very hot, about 3 minutes. Carefully whisk in the flour a little at a time until all the flour is incorporated. (The mixture will foam up as you add the flour, so add a small amount at a time.) Reduce the heat to medium and stir continuously, preferably with a flat-edged wooden spoon, for 22 to 25 minutes, until the roux is a dark brown. To prevent the roux from cooking any further, carefully pour it into a heat-proof bowl and cool for 45 minutes. Drain off any oil that separates from the roux.

Store the roux in a covered container and refrigerate.

BLOND ROUX

MAKES 1 CUP

1 cup unsalted butter
1¼ cups all-purpose flour

Heat butter in a 3-quart saucepan over high heat until very hot, about 2 minutes. Carefully whisk in the flour a little at a time until all the flour is incorporated. (The mixture will foam up as you add the flour, so add a small amount at a time.) Reduce the heat to medium and stir continuously, preferably with a flat-edged wooden spoon, for 10 to 13 minutes, until the roux is a golden brown. To prevent the roux from cooking any further, carefully pour it into a heat-proof bowl and cool for 45 minutes. Drain off any oil that separates from the roux.

Store the roux in a covered container and refrigerate.

Note
Warning! This stuff is HOT when it gets to the dark-brown stage. If you splash it on yourself, it will leave a nasty burn!

SEASONED FLOUR

MAKES 1¼ CUPS

1 cup all-purpose flour
3 tablespoons cornstarch
2 teaspoons Angel Dust Cajun Seasoning
  (page 137)
¼ teaspoon salt
⅛ teaspoon garlic salt
⅛ teaspoon onion salt
⅛ teaspoon freshly ground black pepper
⅛ teaspoon ground white pepper

Whisk all ingredients together in a small bowl. Store in an airtight container and refrigerate. The mix can be kept for months in the refrigerator.

SEASONED CORN FLOUR

MAKES 1½ CUPS

1¼ cups corn flour (see note)
3 tablespoons cornstarch
1 tablespoon Angel Dust Cajun Seasoning
  (page 137)
¾ teaspoon salt
⅛ teaspoon Hungarian paprika
⅛ teaspoon Spanish paprika
⅛ teaspoon onion salt
⅛ teaspoon garlic salt
⅛ teaspoon freshly ground black pepper
⅛ teaspoon ground white pepper

Whisk all ingredients together in a small bowl. Store in an airtight container in the refrigerator.

Note
Corn flour is a more refined version of cornmeal. It has no grit.

ITALIAN BREAD CRUMBS

MAKES 2½ CUPS

8 large fresh basil leaves
2 cups dried bread crumbs
½ cup grated Parmesan cheese
1 tablespoon minced fresh parsley
2 teaspoons Angel Dust Cajun Seasoning
  (page 137)
½ teaspoon garlic salt
½ teaspoon salt

Place the basil leaves between 2 paper towels
and transfer to a microwave oven. Cook on
high power for 15 seconds, or until basil is dry.
Cool and crumble up.

Mix the basil with the remaining ingredients
and store in an airtight container.

Note
*If a microwave oven is unavailable, dry the basil
on a cookie sheet in a conventional oven without
the paper towels at 250° for 5 to 8 minutes.*

JAPANESE BREAD CRUMBS

MAKES ¾ CUP

½ cup dried bread crumbs
¼ cup panko bread crumbs (see note)
1½ teaspoons Angel Dust Cajun Seasoning
  (page 137)

Combine all ingredients in a small bowl. Store
in an airtight container in the refrigerator.
They can keep for several months.

Note
*These Japanese bread crumbs, available in most
Asian markets, are flaky and coarse. They produce
an extra-crispy crust.*

ANGEL DUST CAJUN SEASONING

MAKES ½ CUP

3 tablespoons Hungarian paprika
1½ tablespoons Spanish paprika
5 teaspoons salt
1¼ teaspoons dried thyme leaves
1¼ teaspoons dried oregano
1 teaspoon ground white pepper
½ teaspoon dried basil
½ teaspoon cayenne pepper
¼ teaspoon freshly ground black pepper
⅛ teaspoon garlic powder
⅛ teaspoon onion powder

Combine all ingredients in a small bowl until thoroughly mixed. Store in an airtight container. The spice mix keeps its best flavor for about two months. It is also available from our website, *heavenonseven.com.*

Note
This recipe could easily be doubled and stored for future use.

DRY RUB JERK SEASONING

MAKES ½ CUP

2 tablespoons onion powder
1 tablespoon ground allspice
1 tablespoon ground thyme
2 teaspoons ground cinnamon
2 teaspoons ground cloves
1 teaspoon granulated sugar
1 teaspoon ground coriander
1 teaspoon ground habanero chile powder
1 teaspoon freshly ground black pepper
1 teaspoon garlic powder
½ teaspoon Hungarian paprika
½ teaspoon ground nutmeg
¼ teaspoon salt

Combine all the ingredients in a small bowl. Store in an airtight container. The mix can be kept for up to two months.

JIMMY'S JAMAICAN JERK MARINADE

MAKES ¾ CUP

2 tablespoons ground allspice
½ teaspoon ground nutmeg
½ teaspoon ground cinnamon
¼ teaspoon ground cloves
½ cup sliced green onion, white
    and green parts
1 tablespoon seeded, chopped habanero
    chile
1½ teaspoons minced garlic
2 tablespoons fresh thyme leaves
2 tablespoons freshly squeezed Key lime,
    or regular lime juice
2 tablespoons canola oil
1 tablespoon soy sauce
1 tablespoon dark rum
1½ teaspoons peeled, grated fresh ginger
1½ teaspoons honey
1½ teaspoons cane syrup or light molasses
1½ teaspoons freshly ground black pepper
1 teaspoon dark brown sugar
¾ teaspoon Worcestershire sauce
½ teaspoon habanero hot pepper sauce
¼ teaspoon salt
⅛ teaspoon crushed red pepper flakes

Prepare the marinade by adding the allspice, nutmeg, cinnamon, and cloves to a small skillet. Heat the spices over medium-low heat for 45 to 60 seconds, stirring frequently. Transfer to a coffee grinder and grind to a fine powder. Put the spice mixture and the remaining ingredients into a blender and purée into a thick paste. Store in a covered container and refrigerate for up to a week.

BALSAMIC REDUCTION

MAKES ½ CUP

1 cup balsamic vinegar
2 tablespoons plus 1 teaspoon granulated
    sugar

Combine vinegar and sugar in a small saucepan. Bring to a boil over medium-high heat and simmer 15 minutes, until syrupy and reduced by two thirds. Use at room temperature, or refrigerate and rewarm gently to serve.

CHICKEN STOCK

MAKES 4 QUARTS

7 pounds chicken bones, rinsed (any
   combination of backs, necks, and
   wing tips)
6 quarts water
2 cups coarsely chopped yellow onion
2 cups coarsely chopped celery
2 cups coarsely chopped carrot
6 sprigs parsley
6 stems fresh thyme
2 bay leaves
1 teaspoon kosher salt
½ teaspoon whole black peppercorns

Place the bones in a 16-quart stockpot and
cover with the water. Add the onion, celery,
carrot, parsley, thyme, bay leaves, salt, and peppercorns, and bring to a boil over high heat.
Reduce the heat to medium-low and simmer,
partially covered, for 4 hours. During the first
15 minutes of simmering, skim away any of
the foam and impurities that rise to the surface. Check the bones occasionally to make
sure they are still covered with water; if not,
add water to cover.

Cool, strain, and store in 1-quart containers in
the refrigerator. Remove any fat that collects on
the surface. Store unused stock in the freezer.

Note
*This makes more than most people use at one time.
Since you're spending 4 hours on this, it makes
sense to prepare a larger quantity than you need.
Freeze leftover stock in small containers, and use
it to make gumbo, soup, gravy, and sauces that call
for chicken stock. The possibilities are endless!*

Veal Stock

7 pounds veal shank bones, cut into 2-inch pieces

2 pounds chicken bones, rinsed (any combination of backs, necks, and wing tips)

4 cups coarsely chopped yellow onion

2 cups coarsely chopped celery

2 cups coarsely chopped carrot

4 large plum tomatoes, cut in half

1 cup dry red wine

6 quarts water

¼ cup tomato paste

5 cloves peeled garlic

10 sprigs parsley

5 stems fresh thyme

2 bay leaves

½ teaspoon whole black peppercorns

Preheat the oven to 450°. Arrange the racks in the oven to allow for two large shallow roasting pans. Place the veal bones in one of the roasting pans and roast on the lower rack for 1 hour. Move the pan with the veal bones to the top rack. Put the chicken bones in the second pan, place on the lower oven rack and roast for 30 minutes. Add the onion, celery, carrot, and tomatoes to the roasting pans and toss with some of the rendered fat from the chicken bones. Roast for 30 minutes. Carefully transfer the bones and vegetables to a 16-quart stockpot. Drain excess fat from the roasting pans, place pans on the stovetop over medium-high heat, and deglaze each pan with half the wine and a little of the water, scraping up any browned meat particles into the liquid. Pour into the stockpot along with the remaining water. Add the tomato paste, garlic, parsley, thyme, bay leaves, and peppercorns, and bring to a boil over high heat. Reduce the heat to medium-low and simmer, partially covered, for 6 hours. During the first 15 minutes of simmering, skim away any foam and impurities that rise to the surface. Check the bones occasionally to make sure they are still covered with water; if not, add water to cover.

Cool, strain, and store in 1-quart containers in the refrigerator. Remove any fat that collects on the surface. Store unused stock in the freezer.

Note

It is necessary to roast the bones and vegetables to ensure a rich, dark, gelatinous stock

SHRIMP STOCK

MAKES 1 QUART

2 teaspoons extra virgin olive oil
4 cups shrimp shells
5½ cups water
1 cup coarsely chopped yellow onion
½ cup coarsely chopped celery
2 sprigs parsley
2 stems fresh thyme
6 whole black peppercorns
¼ teaspoon kosher salt

Heat the oil in a 4-quart saucepan over high heat and sauté the shells until they turn bright red, about 2 minutes. Add the water, onion, celery, parsley, thyme, peppercorns, and salt, and bring to a boil. Reduce the heat to medium-low and simmer uncovered for 30 minutes.

Cool, strain, and store in several containers in the refrigerator. Remove any fat that collects on the surface. Store unused stock in the freezer.

SHREDDED SMOKED PORK SHOULDER BUTT

MAKES 5 CUPS

2¾-pound smoked boneless pork
   shoulder butt
1 3-ounce package crab boil in a bag
1 tablespoon Angel Dust Cajun Seasoning
   (page 137)
Hot tap water

Place the pork, crab boil, and Cajun seasoning in a 5-quart Dutch oven. Add enough hot tap water to completely cover the meat. Put the lid on the pot and bring to a boil over high heat. Reduce the heat to medium-low and simmer for 2 hours, adding hot water as needed to keep the meat immersed. Drain and cool slightly. Cut the meat into several pieces and place in the bowl of a food processor. Pulse on and off a few times until the meat is broken up. Process for another 20 to 30 seconds, or until the meat is finely shredded. Keep refrigerated, or store unused meat in freezer bags in ½- to 1-cup portions in the freezer.

Note

Crab boil is a New Orleans seasoning mix used to boil shrimp and crawfish as well as crabs. Good brands include Rex and Zatarain's.

ROASTED-GARLIC PURÉE (AND GARLIC OIL)

1 cup peeled garlic cloves
1 cup extra virgin or regular olive oil

Preheat the oven to 300°.

Place the garlic in a small ovenproof container and pour in the oil. Use additional oil if needed to completely immerse all the garlic cloves. Cover the container with aluminum foil and roast 1 hour, until garlic is soft and light golden brown.

Strain the garlic and place in a blender along with 2 tablespoons of the oil. Purée to a smooth consistency, adding a small amount of oil if necessary. Pour into a container and cover the top of the purée with a thin layer of the oil. Cover and store in the refrigerator.

Reserve the remaining garlic-infused oil in another container and refrigerate.

Note
We use roasted garlic in dozens of dishes in my restaurants because I love its unique and nutty flavor. The oil that it's cooked in can be used for sautéing meats or vegetables. This recipe can easily be doubled and stored in the refrigerator for up to one month. Or if you want, you can just slap it on French bread and wolf it down.

ROASTED PEPPERS

Any type, size, or amount of peppers or chiles

For small quantities of peppers, roast each pepper directly over the flame of a stovetop burner. Holding the peppers with tongs, turn the peppers until skin is blistered. Depending on size, each pepper will take from 2 to 5 minutes.

For large quantities of peppers, heat the broiler. Line the broiler pan with aluminum foil. Roast similar-sized peppers under the broiler until well blistered, but not completely blackened. Turn the peppers with tongs to char them evenly; this takes 8 to 12 minutes per batch.

Place the peppers in a plastic resealable bag and close tightly, or place in a bowl and cover with plastic wrap. Cool 20 minutes. Peel away and discard the charred skin, seeds, and stems. Roasted peppers can be stored for several days in the refrigerator.

INDEX

DATE DUE

Demco, Inc. 38-293

Clackamas County Library
16201 S.E. McLoughlin Blvd.
Oak Grove, OR 97267

JUL 1 0 2001